BON APPÉTIT
OUTDOOR
ENTERTAINING

BON APPÉTIT

OUTDOOR ENTERTAINING

FROM THE EDITORS OF BON APPÉTIT

CONDÉ NAST BOOKS / PANTHEON   NEW YORK

For Bon Appétit Magazine

William Garry, Editor-in-Chief
Laurie Glenn Buckle, Editor, Bon Appétit Books
Marcy MacDonald, Editorial Business Manager
Carri Marks, Editorial Production Director
Sybil Shimazu Neubauer, Editorial Administrator
Jordana Ruhland, Assistant Editor
Marcia Lewis, Editorial Support
James Badham, Text
Siobhan Burns, Supplemental Text
H. Abigail Bok, Copy Editor
Gaylen Ducker Grody, Research
Jeanne Thiel Kelley, Food Research

For Condé Nast Books

Lisa Faith Phillips, Vice President and General Manager
Tom Downing, Associate Direct Marketing Director
Lucille Friedman, Fulfillment Manager
Colleen P. Shire, Assistant Direct Marketing Manager
Angela Lee, Direct Marketing Associate
Meredith L. Peters, Direct Marketing Assistant

Produced in association with Patrick Filley Associates, Inc.

Designed by Joel Avirom and Jason Snyder

Front Jacket: Pineapple, Apricot and Cherry Pies (page 76).

ISBN 0-375-40767-7

Manufactured in Hong Kong

FIRST EDITION

2 4 6 8 9 7 5 3 1

Condé Nast Web Address: http://www.epicurious.com

Random House Web Address: http://www.randomhouse.com

CONTENTS

INTRODUCTION

*W*hat's trite is often true, and the old saw that food tastes better outdoors is without a doubt both. Think back to that juicy hamburger you devoured at a beach barbecue as a kid; or that grilled fish you enjoyed while watching a tropical sunset from a breezy deck; or that warming cup of soup you sipped on a long chair lift ride up a ski mountain. Could that food have tasted any better? Probably not: Because the one ingredient common to that particular burger, that extraordinary fish dinner, and that memorable serving of soup was none other than the great outdoors.

Being out in the air—whether in a garden, on a terrace, at the beach or by a mountain stream—awakens the senses, including those of smell and taste; so it's not surprising that everything tastes better under a big sky. Having breakfast, brunch, lunch or dinner outside also adds an element of fun and adventure to the gathering. It doesn't matter if the site is a hidden cove on a distant beach or just the deck around your back-yard swimming pool, an outdoor party holds a special appeal for hosts and guests alike. There is the sense that something different is happening, and that makes things all the more intriguing.

We begin this book with a few simple premises: The first is that bringing people together to enjoy food and drink at an appealing outdoor location is a good and desirable thing to do; the second is that just about anyone can use a little help from *Bon Appétit* when it comes to handling the details, whether it's figuring out just what kind of party to have, coming up with a theme, settling on a menu or getting the food on the table; and the third and perhaps most important premise is that easier is always better.

In the following almost two hundred pages, we provide you with more than two dozen ideas for simple yet stylish outdoor meals that range from an intimate romantic picnic for two to a block party for fifty. But we don't just give you the idea and a few recipes and call it quits. Nope; we bolster the notion with shopping, planning and decorating tips, do-ahead advice, serving suggestions *and* menu after menu of recipes that are exactly what you want for an outdoor occasion.

To make things even more approachable for novice entertainers and old pros alike, we have divided the book into three sections. In the first, we present ideas for outdoor parties: lunch on the terrace, an alfresco dinner, a big back-yard barbecue, a pool party and more. Your kitchen may be nearby, giving you access to everything you need, be it the stove or a blender, but the fact that you are out-of-doors makes the occasion that much more special.

These parties are both casual and sophisticated, intimate and expansive. They include a lovely brunch with made-to-order omelets and an elegant dinner of herb-marinated and grilled veal chops that you might serve on the terrace or patio. There's a big steak barbecue for sixteen and a family get-together for twenty that's made simple with a recipe for chili that you serve in individual hollowed-out loaves of bread (fewer dishes to wash!).

The last section of the book features ideas, menus and recipes for truly movable feasts—food you pack up to take with you to the beach, to the concert or the campsite, even on a bicycle trip or a day of cross-country skiing. Now, a lot of people, whenever they leave home and know that they have to pack a picnic, switch into ordinary-sandwich mode. Nothing wrong with that (even a PB&J tastes better outdoors); but once you see how simple it is to create a truly satisfying spread for a tailgate picnic or an afternoon at the lake, your motto may well change from "Less is more" to "Have great food, will travel." You'll be surprised just how delicious, stylish and easy these picnics are.

We tell you how to pack food safely (it's not complicated at all), how much to take, what essential tools and implements you'll need and how to minimize the preparation required as you break out lunch, say, while sitting by the side of a stream. (One example: A cake designed for an outing can be cut into satisfyingly big pieces and wrapped individually for easier serving on the road.) We've thought of everything, so you don't have to worry about forgetting anything.

Sandwiched between the Parties and Picnics sections is the incredibly useful Sourcebook. It's packed with recipes that are ideal for outdoor entertaining, from fast and tasty salads to the best barbecued steaks, ribs and more. Mix and match these recipes within the book's menus, or create your own menus, beginning with a dish so appealing you find yourself firing up the grill before you've even finished reading the recipe (how does grilled pork tenderloin with roasted garlic butter sound? Ribs with mustard-bourbon sauce? Grilled swordfish tostadas with black beans?). In addition, the Sourcebook is a wealth of information relevant to dining in the great outdoors, from a primer on grilling to picnic-packing ideas that take you "beyond the basket."

We haven't limited our stash of good ideas, useful information and entertaining hints to the Sourcebook, though. Throughout the book you'll find 20 sidebars that cover aspects of the various parties and picnics in more detail. Where do you start when planning a block party? Any clever ideas for setting a stylish but casual outdoor table? How do you go about renting enough glasses for eighteen guests? Check the sidebars for all the answers.

What it all adds up to is a complete package for entertaining under the sun or under the stars, on the beach or in the back yard. Virtually everything you need to know is contained in this detail-filled, leave-no-stone-unturned, everything-is-thought-of book. With beautiful photographs that extend the subject matter by setting the mood and offering more serving and set-up ideas, this book really covers the territory.

So pick your spot, select a menu (or mix and match the recipes as you see fit), call up some folks and make a date. We'll help you see everything through to a memorable occasion that will add new meaning to the term *the great outdoors*.

PARTIES

Collectively, herbs are one of the great pleasures of life. They taste good, they smell good, they are often beautiful. The very idea of an herb garden conjures up images of a slightly wild, especially fragrant plot bordered by stone walls, shaded by old trees—the perfect place for a late-morning meal. But you don't need an herb garden to pull off this menu, just a lovely outdoor location, a nice day and these herb-scented recipes, which can serve as reminders of gardens known, visited or imagined.

Brunch is a meal that presupposes a leisurely weekend pace. And because it is often celebratory and is always served well after the crack of dawn, it carries the expectation of a little indulgence: late rising; an extra cup of coffee; a light cocktail; a chance to read the paper, do the crossword and enjoy some great-tasting food—slowly, with family or friends.

This brunch features made-to-order omelets (the eggs flecked with chives and tarragon), Champagne cocktails, a platter of sliced melon and prosciutto, and a lovely Mediterranean-style salad of sliced fennel, arugula and oranges. For dessert, treat your guests (and yourself) to individual bread puddings made with croissants and studded with chopped chocolate. It's a menu that won't leave anyone overworked or underfed. But unlike one of those enormous hotel brunches, it's sensible, too—not too much, not too little: in other words, just right.

SMOKED SALMON OMELETS WITH HERBS

FOR A PERFECT omelet, use a nonstick skillet and a heatproof rubber spatula. Any omelet that is not quite set in the center after cooking on the stove can be finished in a preheated 350°F oven for just a few minutes.

6 SERVINGS

½	cup sour cream
3	tablespoons coarse-grained Dijon mustard
12	large eggs
⅓	cup water
6	tablespoons finely chopped fresh chives or green onion tops
¼	cup minced fresh tarragon
6	teaspoons butter
6	ounces smoked salmon, cut into strips

Preheat oven to 250°F. Whisk sour cream and mustard in medium bowl to blend. Whisk eggs, ⅓ cup water, chives and tarragon in large bowl to blend. Season mixture with salt and pepper.

Melt 1 teaspoon butter in small nonstick skillet over medium-high heat. Add scant ½ cup of egg mixture and stir briefly. Let eggs begin to set at edges. Using spatula, lift edges and tilt pan, allowing uncooked portion to flow underneath. Cook until eggs are set but still moist, about 1 minute. Spread scant 2 tablespoons of mustard mixture and ⅙ of salmon over half of omelet. Using spatula, fold unfilled portion over filling. Slide omelet out onto baking sheet. Keep warm in oven. Repeat with remaining butter, egg mixture, mustard mixture and smoked salmon to make remaining omelets. Transfer omelets to plates and serve.

PEACH CHAMPAGNE COCKTAIL

THIS REFRESHING cocktail makes a great start to brunch, along with a platter of prosciutto-wrapped wedges of melon.

MAKES ABOUT 10 CUPS

4	cups fresh orange juice
2	cups vodka
1	cup peach schnapps
1	chilled 750-ml bottle brut Champagne or other sparkling wine
	Ice cubes
	Fresh mint sprigs
	Sliced fresh peaches

Mix first 3 ingredients in large pitcher. *(Can be prepared 4 hours ahead. Cover and refrigerate. Stir before continuing.)* Add Champagne to orange juice mixture. Fill tall glasses with ice. Pour orange juice mixture over. Garnish glasses with mint sprigs and peach slices.

FENNEL, ARUGULA AND ORANGE SALAD

As SIMPLE AS this salad is, it's surpisingly elegant. Whip up the orange juice and balsamic dressing the day before, if you like.

6 SERVINGS

2½	tablespoons fresh orange juice
2	tablespoons olive oil
1	tablespoon balsamic vinegar
6	cups trimmed, cored, thinly sliced fennel bulbs (about 3 large)
2	bunches arugula (about 3 cups)
3	large oranges, peel and white pith removed, cut into ½-inch pieces
1½	ounces pecorino Romano cheese, shaved

Whisk first 3 ingredients in small bowl. *(Can be prepared 1 day ahead; chill. Rewhisk before using.)*

Combine fennel, arugula, oranges and cheese in large bowl; add dressing and toss to coat. Season salad with salt and pepper.

CHOCOLATE CROISSANT BREAD PUDDINGS

INCREDIBLY RICH—and worth every calorie. Make these individual puddings up to three hours ahead, in the cool of the morning.

6 SERVINGS

2	large croissants (about 6 ounces total), cut into ½-inch cubes
5	ounces bittersweet (not unsweetened) or semisweet chocolate, chopped
2	cups whipping cream
½	vanilla bean, split lengthwise
4	large egg yolks
½	cup sugar

Preheat oven to 350°F. Arrange croissant cubes on large baking sheet. Bake until golden brown, about 10 minutes. Remove from oven; cool. Reduce oven temperature to 325°F.

Divide chocolate among six ¾-cup custard cups. Top with croissant cubes, dividing equally. Pour 2 cups cream into heavy medium saucepan. Scrape in seeds from vanilla bean; add bean. Bring to simmer over medium heat. Remove from heat. Whisk egg yolks and sugar in medium bowl to blend. Gradually whisk in hot cream mixture. Discard vanilla bean. Pour custard over chocolate and croissants, dividing equally.

Place cups in large baking pan. Add enough water to pan to come halfway up sides of cups.

Bake puddings until set, about 40 minutes. Remove from water; cool slightly. *(Can be prepared up to 3 hours ahead. Cover loosely; keep at room temperature.)* Serve warm or at room temperature.

COLD ARTICHOKE AND LEEK SOUP

PASTA SALAD WITH TUNA
AND BLACK OLIVES

ROSEMARY TOASTS

ICED TEA OR DRY WHITE WINE

MOCHA MOUSSE CAKE

Menu for Six

*I*nterior designers like to talk about "bringing the outside in." A terrace or deck essentially does the opposite—extending the framework of a house or apartment *outward* to provide a comfortable, welcoming setting in a garden, on a rooftop, by a pool, even high above—and at a comfortable remove from—a city street.

The terrace is a special setting, and it calls for a special lunch. Guests feel unfettered and instantly comfortable outdoors. The terrace also lends itself to informality, especially at lunch, and that takes the pressure off the busy host or hostess.

This menu for a terrace lunch is a snap, as it's made up of make-ahead recipes, most of them offered either chilled or at room temperature. The creamy soup, which combines artichokes and leeks, can be served straight from the refrigerator. The pasta salad, a flavorful mix of fusilli, fresh tuna, sun-dried tomatoes and Kalamata olives, needs to cool, so there's no last-minute rushing there. That leaves only the super-simple rosemary toasts to broil just before lunch. And if your guests polish off the do-ahead mocha mousse cake (an ingenious layering of chocolate-espresso mousse and chocolate wafers that sets up overnight in the refrigerator) for dessert, no problem: It's just one less thing to bring from the outside in.

COLD ARTICHOKE AND LEEK SOUP

FROZEN ARTICHOKE hearts, leeks, chicken broth and sour cream combine to make an elegant—yet easy—start to lunch. Prepare this a day ahead of time and serve it straight from the refrigerator.

6 SERVINGS

2 9-ounce packages frozen artichoke hearts, thawed

4 teaspoons butter

2 cups (packed) sliced leeks (white part only)

5 cups canned low-salt chicken broth

½ cup sour cream

Chopped fresh chives

Finely chop artichokes in processor using on/off turns. Melt butter in heavy large saucepan over medium heat. Add leeks and sauté until tender, about 10 minutes. Add artichoke hearts and sauté 2 minutes. Add broth; bring to boil. Reduce heat, cover and simmer 15 minutes. Thoroughly puree soup in processor. Strain soup through sieve set over bowl, forcing solids through with rubber spatula to extract as much puree as possible. Return puree to saucepan. Add sour cream and whisk until smooth. Season to taste with salt and pepper. Cover and refrigerate until cold, about 3 hours. *(Can be prepared 1 day ahead. Keep refrigerated.)* Sprinkle with chives and serve.

PASTA SALAD WITH TUNA AND BLACK OLIVES

6 SERVINGS

1 pound fusilli pasta

7 tablespoons olive oil

4 garlic cloves, finely chopped

¾ cup thinly sliced drained oil-packed sun-dried tomatoes (about 4 ounces)

4 5-ounce tuna steaks (each 1 inch thick)

1 cup chopped fresh basil

½ cup chopped fresh Italian parsley

6 tablespoons balsamic vinegar

⅓ cup chopped pitted Kalamata olives or other brine-cured black olives

2 tablespoons drained capers

Cook fusilli in large pot of boiling salted water until tender but still firm to bite. Drain. Transfer to large bowl. Toss with 2 tablespoons oil.

Heat 3 tablespoons oil in heavy large skillet over medium heat. Add garlic and sauté until fragrant, about 1 minute. Stir in tomatoes. Add to pasta; cool slightly. *(Can be prepared 1 day ahead. Cover and refrigerate. Bring pasta to room tem-perature before continuing with recipe.)*

Prepare barbecue (medium-high heat) or preheat broiler. Brush tuna with 2 tablespoons oil. Sprinkle with salt and pepper. Grill or broil tuna until cooked to desired doneness, about 4 minutes per side for medium. Cut crosswise into ⅓-inch-thick slices. Add to pasta.

Add basil and all remaining ingredients to pasta; toss. Season with salt and pepper.

ROSEMARY TOASTS

IN THIS SIMPLE recipe, an herb-flavored oil is brushed on sliced Italian bread, which gets broiled. Other herbs—such as tarragon, thyme or basil—would also work well.

6 SERVINGS

6	tablespoons olive oil (preferably extra-virgin)
2	tablespoons chopped fresh rosemary or 2 teaspoons dried
3	large garlic cloves, minced
12	½-inch-thick diagonal slices crusty Italian bread (each about 3 x 5 inches)

Preheat broiler. Stir oil, rosemary and garlic in small saucepan over low heat until fragrant, about 2 minutes. Season with salt and pepper.

Arrange bread slices on large baking sheet. Broil until golden, about 1 minute. Turn toasts over. Brush with oil mixture, dividing equally. Broil toasts until golden and crisp, approximately 1 minute. Serve toasts warm.

MOCHA MOUSSE CAKE

THIS EASY DO-AHEAD dessert takes its inspiration from the classic Italian sweet tiramisù.

6 SERVINGS

4	ounces cream cheese, room temperature
¼	cup sugar
1	tablespoon instant espresso powder
1	teaspoon vanilla extract
1¼	cups whipping cream
27	chocolate wafer cookies
2	ounces bittersweet (not unsweetened) or semisweet chocolate, grated

Line 8 x 4-inch loaf pan with plastic wrap. Using electric mixer, beat first 4 ingredients in large bowl until smooth. Beat in ¼ cup cream. Whip remaining 1 cup cream in another large bowl until medium-soft peaks form. Fold into coffee mixture. Spread ½ cup mousse evenly over bottom of prepared pan. Place 1 cookie on clean surface. Spread with about 1 tablespoon mousse. Top with cookie. Repeat until 3 stacks of 9 cookies each are made, with cookie on bottom and top of each stack. Place stacks on sides atop mousse in pan. Fill pan with remaining mousse. Cover with plastic; chill overnight.

Remove plastic from top of pan. Invert mousse cake onto platter. Remove remaining plastic. Garnish top with grated chocolate.

CHAMPAGNE

BEET DIP WITH FRESH VEGETABLES

HERBED CHEESE STRAWS

CURRIED PORK AND ONION SKEWERS
WITH MANGO-PINEAPPLE SALSA

GREEN BEANS WITH CASHEWS
AND SESAME SEEDS

STEAMED WHITE RICE

GAMAY BEAUJOLAIS

GLAZED PLUM CHEESECAKES

Menu for Eighteen

Celebration? Now, there's a word that puts people in the mood for a party. And whether you plan to help a couple renew their wedding vows, toast a promotion, warm a new house or just rejoice at the arrival of spring, an outdoor gathering for eighteen, made up of lovely, simply prepared dishes, should do the trick nicely.

This easy-to-make menu stars tropical and Asian flavors perfectly suited to warm-weather dining. And here's another enticement: Everything but the grilling of the curried pork skewers can be done well ahead of time. For starters, set out bowls of the pretty-in-pink beet dip with an assortment of fresh vegetables, adding herbed cheese straws (made quickly with purchased frozen puff pastry) to the mix for crunch and pouring Champagne to set the right tone. The skewers, which take just ten minutes to cook, are served with a beautiful mango and pineapple salsa, along with rice and a green bean and cashew salad (prepare it several hours ahead and let stand at room temperature). For dessert, it's as easy to make two cheesecakes as it is one, these topped with glazed fresh plums. Bake them the day before the party, refrigerate overnight, then add the fruit topping early the next morning. After that, there's little left to do but, well, celebrate.

CELEBRATION LUNCH

HERBED CHEESE STRAWS

MAKES ABOUT 44

- 1 cup packed chilled grated Parmesan cheese (about 3 ounces)
- ¾ cup packed chilled grated white cheddar cheese (about 3 ounces)
- 1 tablespoon dried thyme
- 1 sheet frozen puff pastry (half of 17¼-ounce package), thawed

Position rack in center of oven and preheat to 425°F. Line 3 heavy large baking sheets with parchment. Grind both cheeses and thyme in processor until coarse powder forms. Transfer cheese mixture to small bowl.

Place pastry on lightly floured surface. Roll out pastry to 11 x 18-inch rectangle. Arrange pastry so that 1 long side is parallel to edge of work surface. Cover right half of pastry with ⅓ of cheese mixture. Fold left half of pastry over, covering cheese completely; press lightly all over to seal. Repeat rolling to 11 x 18-inch rectangle, sprinkling with ⅓ of cheese, folding and pressing 2 more times (for a total of 3 times; let pastry rest a few minutes if difficult to roll). Roll dough to 11 x 18-inch rectangle. Cut in half crosswise, forming two 11 x 9-inch pieces. Cut dough pieces crosswise into about twenty-two ½-inch-wide by 9-inch-long strips. Twist each strip a few times and place on prepared sheets, pressing ends onto parchment and spacing evenly.

Bake cheese straws until golden, about 8 minutes. Cool 5 minutes. Serve warm or at room temperature. *(Can be made 2 days ahead. Store in airtight container at room temperature. Rewarm in 350°F oven 5 minutes, if desired.)*

BEET DIP WITH FRESH VEGETABLES

GO ALL OUT with Champagne and a spectacular hors d'oeuvres platter including this beet dip, a colorful selection of fresh vegetables and the cheese straws at right.

MAKES 4½ CUPS

- 6 2-inch-diameter beets
- 1 cup chopped red onion
- ¾ cup sour cream
- ¾ cup plain yogurt
- ¾ cup chopped fresh dill
- 4 large garlic cloves, minced

  Assorted fresh vegetables

Cook beets in large pot of boiling salted water until tender, about 35 minutes. Drain; cool. Peel beets and chop coarsely.

Combine beets and onion in processor; blend until smooth. Transfer beet mixture to medium bowl. Mix in sour cream, yogurt, dill and garlic. Season dip to taste with salt and pepper. Cover and refrigerate 2 days.

Spoon dip into bowl. Place on platter. Surround with vegetables and serve.

CURRIED PORK AND ONION SKEWERS WITH MANGO-PINEAPPLE SALSA

THESE FLAVORFUL pork skewers can be marinated overnight. Grill them just before serving. White rice makes a good side dish.

18 SERVINGS

MARINADE

- 4 cups plain nonfat yogurt
- 2 cups chopped fresh cilantro
- 1 cup chopped red onion
- 1 cup Major Grey mango chutney
- 3 generous tablespoons curry powder

PORK

- 4½ pounds pork tenderloin, cut into 72 equal pieces
- 4 red onions, peeled, cut into 72 equal pieces
- 18 10- to 12-inch wooden skewers, soaked 15 minutes in cold water

    Mango-Pineapple Salsa (see recipe at right)

FOR MARINADE: Combine yogurt, cilantro, 1 cup chopped red onion, chutney and curry powder in large bowl. Set marinade aside.

FOR PORK: Alternate 4 pork cubes and 4 red onion pieces on each skewer. Brush with yogurt marinade. Arrange skewers in 13 x 9 x 2-inch baking dishes. Cover and chill at least 2 hours or up to 1 day, turning occasionally.

Prepare barbecue (medium-high heat) or preheat broiler. Grill or broil until pork is brown and just cooked through, turning occasionally, about 10 minutes. Serve with salsa.

MANGO-PINEAPPLE SALSA

TERRIFIC WITH the pork skewers, this would also be good with grilled fish.

MAKES ABOUT 7 CUPS

- 3 large mangoes, peeled, chopped
- 1 pound tomatillos,* husked, rinsed, chopped
- 1 cup chopped fresh cilantro
- 2 tablespoons minced jalapeño chilies
- 2 tablespoons fresh lime juice
- 2 large garlic cloves, minced
- 2 cups chopped peeled pineapple

Combine first 6 ingredients in large bowl. *(Can be made 1 day ahead. Cover; chill.)*

Add pineapple to salsa. Season to taste with salt and pepper. Let stand at least 1 hour to allow flavors to blend.

*Tomatillos, green tomato-like vegetables with paper-thin husks, are available at Latin American markets, specialty foods stores and some supermarkets.

RENTING IT RIGHT

Basically, just about anything you need for a party can be rented. From the flatware to a tent, all the elements are available; it's just a question of finding a reputable renting company and being clear about what you're looking for. First, check with friends, family and co-workers, gathering names of rental agencies they've used and liked. Then consider your party, what you have and what you'll need.

Perhaps the most commonly rented item is a selection of glassware. While most of us don't mind eating from paper plates, drinking from paper cups often just doesn't seem right, especially when the beverage is wine or Champagne. Make sure that you keep your own glasses separate from the rented ones; packing up will be much easier this way.

If you're hosting a sit-down lunch or dinner for a large group, consider renting folding tables and chairs, and the necessary linens.

Finally, a tent can make an outdoor party more comfortable and, so, more successful. It can provide shade on a sunny day or cover if the weather is not cooperating, and at night, it's easy to light and decorate. You may need to contact a company that specializes in tents, and they should be able to give you referrals and brochures. They'll also provide heaters, lighting or fans, as necessary. And plan ahead, especially if your party will be held over a holiday weekend or during the June wedding season.

GREEN BEANS
WITH CASHEWS
AND SESAME SEEDS

SERVED AT ROOM temperature, this side dish can be made several hours ahead of time. Roasted cashews add a nice crunch.

18 SERVINGS

3	pounds green beans, trimmed
¼	cup oriental sesame oil
1½	cups roasted salted cashews, chopped
½	cup sesame seeds, lightly toasted

Cook beans in large pot of boiling salted water until crisp-tender, about 6 minutes. Drain well; rinse with cold water and drain again. Return beans to same pot. Add oil; toss to coat. Add cashews and sesame seeds and toss well. Season with salt and pepper. Transfer to serving bowl. *(Can be made 3 hours ahead. Keep at room temperature.)*

GLAZED PLUM
CHEESECAKES

MAKE THESE DELICIOUS cheesecakes a day ahead so that they have plenty of time to chill.

18 SERVINGS

CRUST

22 whole graham crackers (11 ounces)

½ cup (packed) golden brown sugar

½ teaspoon ground cinnamon

Pinch of salt

10 tablespoons unsalted butter, melted

FILLING

6 8-ounce packages cream cheese, room temperature

2 cups sugar

8 large eggs

2 cups sour cream

2 tablespoons finely grated lemon peel

4 teaspoons vanilla extract

PLUMS

1½ cups orange juice

1 cup red currant jelly

½ cup (packed) golden brown sugar

6 ¼-inch-thick slices fresh ginger

12 large ripe red-skinned plums, halved, pitted, cut into ½-inch-thick wedges

FOR CRUST: Preheat oven to 350°F. Lightly butter two 9-inch-diameter springform pans with 2¾-inch-high sides. Combine graham crackers, brown sugar, cinnamon and salt in processor. Process until fine crumbs form. Mix in melted butter. Divide between prepared pans. Pat crumb mixture over bottoms (not sides) of pans. Bake crusts until set and golden, about 10 minutes. Transfer to racks.

FOR FILLING: Reduce oven temperature to 300°F. Using electric mixter, beat 3 packages cream cheese in large bowl until smooth. Beat in 1 cup sugar. Beat in 4 eggs just until blended. Mix in 1 cup sour cream, 1 tablespoon lemon peel and 2 teaspoons vanilla. Pour filling into 1 crust-lined pan. Repeat with remaining cream cheese, sugar, eggs, sour cream, peel and vanilla. Pour filling into second pan.

Bake until sides of cheesecakes puff slightly and centers are just set, about 1 hour 15 minutes. Turn oven off. Leave cakes in oven with door slightly open for 30 minutes.

Transfer cakes to racks. Run small knife between crusts and pans. Cool cakes completely in pans on racks, about 3 hours (cakes may crack slightly as they cool). Cover and refrigerate cheesecakes overnight.

FOR PLUMS: Divide orange juice, jelly, brown sugar and ginger between 2 heavy large skillets, whisking over medium-high heat until jelly dissolves. Add plums, dividing equally. Bring mixture to boil. Reduce heat to medium-low. Cover and simmer gently until plums are just tender but still hold shape, about 3 minutes. Using slotted spoon, transfer plums to 2 large plates; set aside to cool.

Boil cooking liquid until thickened to syrup consistency, about 7 minutes. *(Plums and syrup can be made 4 hours ahead. Cover separately; chill.)*

Release pan sides from cheesecakes. Arrange plums in concentric circles atop cheesecakes, covering completely. Brush some syrup over plums. Cut cakes into wedges. Serve with remaining syrup.

The Margarita is America's favorite cocktail, so it seems only natural to build a cocktail party around this cool, icy drink. The tropical version here—accented by guava and papaya nectars and cream of coconut—is even better thanks to a homemade "sweet-and-sour" mix that can be prepared up to a week ahead.

Complementing the Margaritas is a collection of lively, great-tasting dishes. Arranged buffet style out-of-doors, they'll turn the fest into the fiesta it is meant to be. The filled-pastry treats known as *empanadas* feature a savory pork filling accented with raisins, almonds and chilies. They're fun to make and can be prepared the day before the party. They play nicely against the do-ahead, chili-marinated shrimp. For the taquitos, set out grilled steak, some *queso fresco,* salsa and tortillas, and encourage your friends to go wild. Finally, a touch of *Nuevo Latino* cooking is added to the mix in the form of Brie, papaya and onion quesadillas (make them a couple of hours ahead and bake briefly just before serving).

This is a party with plenty of substance and style, but a piñata or two, maybe even sombreros, and some of those brightly colored cut-paper streamers draped across the yard wouldn't necessarily hurt. And don't forget to pick up a copy of that old rock 'n' roll classic, with only a single, though on this occasion eminently appropriate, lyric: "Tequila."

MARGARITA PARTY

MARGARITAS WITH TROPICAL FRUIT

12 SERVINGS

1½ cups water

1½ cups sugar

1 cup fresh lemon juice

1 cup fresh lime juice

Lime wedges

Sugar

1 to 1½ cups gold tequila

12 tablespoons papaya nectar

12 tablespoons guava nectar

½ cup canned cream of coconut*

16 ice cubes

12 lime slices

Combine 1½ cups water and sugar in large saucepan. Stir over medium heat just until sugar dissolves. Bring to boil. Cool sugar syrup.

Mix syrup, lemon and lime juices in pitcher. Chill sweet-and-sour mix until cold. *(Can be made 1 week ahead. Cover; keep chilled.)* Rub rims of 12 glasses with lime wedges. Dip in sugar.

Combine 1½ cups sweet-and-sour mix, ½ cup (or more, if desired) tequila, 6 tablespoons papaya nectar, 6 tablespoons guava nectar, ¼ cup cream of coconut and 8 ice cubes in blender. Process until blended. Pour into 6 glasses. Repeat with 1½ cups sweet-and-sour mix (reserve remaining sweet-and-sour mix for another time), tequila, both nectars, cream of coconut and ice cubes. Pour into 6 glasses. Garnish each with lime slice.

*Cream of coconut is available in the liquor department of most supermarkets.

PORK PICADILLO EMPANADAS WITH CHIPOTLE SALSA

A POPULAR DISH in many Spanish-speaking countries, *picadillo* consists of pork, beef or veal plus ingredients such as tomatoes, garlic and onions. The picadillo filling in these savory Latin pastries is accented with jalapeño chili, raisins, almonds and spices.

MAKES 24

FILLING

1 tablespoon olive oil

1 12-ounce pork tenderloin, trimmed, cut into ⅓-inch pieces

1 jalapeño chili, minced

2 teaspoons chili powder

2 teaspoons ground cumin

1½ teaspoons ground cinnamon

1 teaspoon ground allspice

½ cup golden raisins

¼ cup fresh lime juice

6 tablespoons chopped toasted almonds

3 tablespoons sour cream

DOUGH

1½ cups all purpose flour

1 cup Masa Harina (corn tortilla mix)*

1 teaspoon baking powder

1 teaspoon salt

½ cup (1 stick) unsalted butter, melted, cooled

½ cup plus 1 tablespoon water

2 large eggs

Chipotle Salsa (see recipe opposite)

Sour cream

FOR FILLING: Heat oil in large nonstick skillet over medium-high heat. Add pork, jalapeño, chili powder, cumin, cinnamon and allspice to skillet and stir 3 minutes. Add raisins and lime juice; boil until almost all liquid evaporates, 1 minute. Remove from heat. Mix in almonds and sour cream. Season with salt and pepper. Cool. *(Can be prepared 1 day ahead. Cover and refrigerate.)*

FOR DOUGH: Butter 2 large baking sheets. Mix flour, Masa Harina, baking powder and salt in large bowl. Stir in melted butter. Whisk ½ cup plus 1 tablespoon water and 1 egg in small bowl to blend. Add to flour mixture; knead in bowl until smooth, pliable dough forms, about 2 minutes. Working with half of dough at a time, roll out on floured surface to ⅛-inch thickness. Using 3¾-inch-diameter biscuit cutter, cut out rounds. Reroll dough scraps and cut out additional rounds to make 12 rounds per dough half.

Whisk remaining egg in small bowl to blend. Place 1 tablespoon filling in center of each dough round. Lightly brush edges with egg. Fold dough over, pressing edges with fork to seal. Place on prepared baking sheets. *(Can be made 1 day ahead. Cover with plastic wrap; chill.)*

Preheat oven to 375°F. Brush empanadas with beaten egg. Bake until light golden, about 25 minutes. Serve with salsa and sour cream.

*Masa Harina is available at Latin American markets and many supermarkets.

CHIPOTLE SALSA

ALSO TERRIFIC with the *taquitos* and quesadillas here—or partnered with tortilla chips. Guacamole is always a welcome addition to the spread, too.

MAKES ABOUT 3 CUPS

3	cups chopped tomatoes
¾	cup chopped fresh cilantro
3	tablespoons fresh lime juice
1½	tablespoons chopped canned chipotle chilies*
1½	teaspoons ground cumin

Combine all ingredients in medium bowl. Season with salt and pepper. *(Can be prepared 8 hours ahead. Cover and chill.)*

* Chipotle chilies canned in spicy tomato sauce are sold at Latin American markets, specialty foods stores and some supermarkets.

STEAK TAQUITOS

12 SERVINGS

3	cups crumbled queso fresco* or mild feta cheese (about 18 ounces)
24	4- to 6-inch corn tortillas
2	pounds skirt steaks, trimmed
	Chipotle Salsa (see recipe on page 29)

Preheat oven to 350°F. Place queso fresco in bowl. Wrap tortillas in foil. Place in oven until heated through, about 15 minutes.

Meanwhile, prepare barbecue (medium-high heat) or preheat broiler. Season steaks generously with salt and pepper. Grill or broil steaks to desired doneness, about 5 minutes per side for medium-rare. Thinly slice steaks across grain. Place in serving bowl.

Arrange bowls of Chipotle Salsa, queso fresco, corn tortillas and steak on table. Allow guests to assemble their own taquitos.

*Queso fresco, *also known as* queso blanco, *is available at Latin American markets and in the dairy section of some supermarkets.*

BRIE, PAPAYA AND ONION QUESADILLAS

A MODERN interpretation of the classic quesadilla, this one is filled with Brie, cilantro, onion and sliced papaya and baked.

12 SERVINGS

1	tablespoon olive oil
½	large onion, thinly sliced
2	to 3 teaspoons minced seeded jalapeño chili
8	6-inch-diameter flour tortillas
8	ounces Brie, diced
½	cup chopped fresh cilantro
½	large papaya, peeled, seeded, thinly sliced crosswise
	Sour cream
	Chipotle Salsa (optional; see recipe on page 29)

Preheat oven to 425°F. Heat oil in medium skillet over medium-high heat. Add onion and jalapeño and sauté until onion is just tender, about 4 minutes; cool slightly.

Arrange 4 tortillas on heavy large baking sheet. Arrange Brie, then cilantro, papaya and onion mixture over tortillas, dividing equally. Top each with another tortilla, pressing to adhere. *(Can be prepared 2 hours ahead. Cover loosely with plastic; keep at cool room temperature.)*

Bake quesadillas until cheese melts and filling is heated through, about 8 minutes. Transfer quesadillas to platters; cut into wedges. Serve, passing sour cream and salsa.

SPICY MARINATED SHRIMP

JALAPEÑO CHILIES and cayenne pepper add a spicy kick to this south-of-the-border dish. Make it a day ahead of the party and refrigerate until ready to serve.

12 SERVINGS

3	pounds uncooked large shrimp, peeled, deveined, tails left intact
¾	cup olive oil
½	cup finely chopped fresh cilantro
¼	cup white wine vinegar
3	tablespoons fresh lemon juice
3	jalapeño chilies, seeded, minced
3	large garlic cloves
¼	teaspoon cayenne pepper
3	large lemons, sliced
1	large red onion, sliced

Bring large pot of water to boil. Add shrimp and cook until pink and opaque, 3 minutes. Using slotted spoon, transfer shrimp to large bowl of ice water. Drain. Place shrimp in large bowl.

Whisk oil and next 6 ingredients in medium bowl to blend. Season with salt and pepper. Pour marinade over shrimp. Toss to coat. Layer shrimp, lemon slices and onion in large glass bowl. Pour any remaining marinade over. Cover and refrigerate 4 hours. *(Can be prepared 1 day ahead. Keep shrimp refrigerated.)*

SETTING UP AN OUTDOOR BUFFET

When setting up a buffet, think about how to make the plate-filling process as easy as possible for your guests. The first item should be a stack of sturdy plates, then the food, starting with the entrée and moving on to the side dishes and the bread. Make sure that each item has one or two large serving utensils. At the end of the buffet, have a basket of flatware, with knives and forks (and spoons, if necessary) wrapped in large napkins.

To add visual interest to the buffet, put the food in containers of different sizes and shapes. Stack telephone books under the tablecloth (inverted large bowls will work too) to serve as risers for some of the serving pieces. Decorate the table with a variety of things, from flowers and produce to seashells and rocks.

If you have the space, set up the beverages on a separate table, a little bit away from the main buffet. In addition to whatever drinks you're serving, you'll likely need ice and tongs, glasses, napkins, long spoons for stirring drinks, a bottle opener and corkscrew, bar rags, lemon and lime slices, a recycling bin and a trash can. If you're expecting a thirsty crowd, keep extra bottles of wine, soda and liquor under the bar or nearby rather than on the bar itself; this will give your guests more room to maneuver.

TAPENADE CAESAR WITH PROSCIUTTO

GRILLED VEAL CHOPS WITH
LEMON-GARLIC RUB

VEGETABLES GLAZED WITH
BALSAMIC VINEGAR

GOAT CHEESE AND FONTINA RISOTTO

PINOT NOIR

ITALIAN HAZELNUT SHORTBREAD
COOKIES

STRAWBERRY AND ORANGE SORBET

CAPPUCCINO

Menu for Six

*A*lfresco is a word that brings to mind much more than simply eating under the sun or stars. It evokes scenes of Italy; of dappled shade under grape arbors; of sun-soaked produce, artisan cheeses and lip-smacking wine so local it has no label. It makes us think of all the joys of the table and their connection to the fields—in places like Tuscany and Piedmont, Lombardy and Emilia-Romagna. It makes us hungry for good company and simple, straightforward, full-flavored food.

Getting to Italy, of course, is not always so easy; but that is no reason not to let thoughts of that country and its cuisine inspire a perfect alfresco meal. This menu for six begins with a Caesar salad embellished by a superb olive-raisin tapenade. Thanks to a do-ahead dressing and pre-washed romaine, it is well suited to no-hassle entertaining.

The salad is followed by veal chops that are as simple as can be: A lemony herb rub is applied ahead of time, and the chops are grilled while a mix of squash, onion and bell peppers is sautéed in olive oil and finished with balsamic vinegar. A short-cut risotto with goat cheese and Fontina rounds out the meal. For dessert, offer the refreshing strawberry and orange sorbet with shortbread cookies flavored with hazelnuts. Cappuccino would wrap things up on just the right note.

TAPENADE CAESAR WITH PROSCIUTTO

THIS INNOVATIVE take on the classic features an intensely flavored olive and raisin *tapenade* that is also great teamed with breadsticks or spread onto *bruschetta*.

6 SERVINGS

TAPENADE

1 cup Kalamata olives or other brine-cured black olives (about 5 ounces), pitted

½ cup raisins

¼ cup chopped fresh parsley

3 canned anchovy fillets, drained

2 medium shallots, sliced

2 tablespoons fresh lemon juice

1 tablespoon fennel seeds

½ teaspoon cayenne pepper

½ cup olive oil

DRESSING

5 tablespoons fresh lemon juice

¼ cup (packed) grated Parmesan cheese

3 tablespoons coarse-grained Dijon mustard

2 tablespoons finely chopped drained canned anchovy fillets

2 tablespoons finely chopped drained capers

2 tablespoons chopped garlic

1 cup olive oil

3 hearts of romaine lettuce, torn into pieces

4 ounces thin prosciutto slices, cut crosswise into strips

Pecorino Romano cheese shavings

FOR TAPENADE: Blend olives, raisins, parsley, anchovies, shallots, lemon juice, fennel seeds and cayenne in processor until almost smooth, occasionally scraping down sides of bowl. With machine running, add oil and process until blended. Season to taste with salt and pepper.

FOR DRESSING: Whisk lemon juice and next 5 ingredients in medium bowl until well blended. Gradually whisk in oil. Season with salt and pepper. *(Tapenade and dressing can be made 2 days ahead. Cover separately; chill. Bring to room temperature before using.)*

Place lettuce in large bowl. Toss with enough dressing to coat generously. Divide lettuce among 6 plates. Dot perimeter of each plate with teaspoonfuls of tapenade. Top each salad with prosciutto and Romano and serve.

GRILLED VEAL CHOPS with LEMON-GARLIC RUB

A SIMPLE "rub" of garlic, lemon peel, paprika and tarragon flavors the veal chops (lamb chops would work well, too). Let them marinate overnight in the refrigerator, then grill them just before serving.

6 SERVINGS

4 large garlic cloves, pressed
4½ tablespoons minced lemon peel (yellow part only)
3 tablespoons paprika
1½ teaspoons dried tarragon
1½ teaspoons black pepper
6 1-inch-thick veal loin or rib chops
  Olive oil

Combine first 5 ingredients in medium bowl. Rub garlic mixture onto both sides of veal. Cover and refrigerate overnight.

Prepare barbecue (medium-high heat). Season veal with salt and drizzle oil over. Grill to desired doneness, about 4 minutes per side for medium-rare. Serve immediately.

VEGETABLES GLAZED with BALSAMIC VINEGAR

A COLORFUL sauté of peppers and squash is enlivened with a splash of balsamic vinegar. While these are best prepared just before serving, the vegetables can be washed and cut up ahead of time and kept in plastic bags in the refrigerator.

6 SERVINGS

3 tablespoons olive oil
1½ red bell peppers, cut into ¼-inch-wide strips
1½ yellow bell peppers, cut into ¼-inch-wide strips
1 medium onion, thinly sliced
3 zucchini, trimmed, cut crosswise into ½-inch-thick rounds
3 yellow summer squash, trimmed, cut crosswise into ½-inch-thick rounds
3 tablespoons balsamic vinegar

Heat oil in heavy large nonstick skillet over medium-high heat. Add peppers and onion. Sauté until beginning to soften, about 4 minutes. Add zucchini and yellow squash and sauté until tender, about 8 minutes. Add vinegar to skillet and boil until liquid is reduced to glaze and coats vegetables, about 2 minutes. Season to taste with salt and pepper. Transfer vegetables to platter and then serve.

GARDEN-INSPIRED CENTERPIECES

One of the joys of dining alfresco is that nothing fancy is required when it comes to decorating the table. There are plenty of simple ways to turn the best of your garden into beautiful centerpieces: a handful of freshly picked flowers in a jam jar; a potted ivy; a bowl of fresh tomatoes or peppers; a basket of beautiful ripe fruit.

If you have a little more time to spare, try one of these quick and easy ideas.

◆ Fill a glass bowl, vase or compote dish with strawberries, limes, cranberries or kumquats, then cover them with water and arrange fresh flowers among them.

◆ In a shallow glass bowl, float large rose blooms or gardenias in a couple of inches of water; you could also place one bloom in each of several small bowls, liqueur glasses or teacups and line them up down the length of the table.

◆ Line the inside of a glass bowl with lemon slices, then fill it with glass beads (available at a florist's or hobby shop). Add water (carefully) and flowers.

◆ Small terra-cotta pots of herbs look right at home on an outdoor table. Tie some ribbon or raffia around each pot, if you like, and cluster a few of them in the center of the table, or march three or four in a line down the middle. These could also serve as gifts for your guests, who will then go home with a reminder of a lovely event.

GOAT CHEESE AND FONTINA RISOTTO

6 SERVINGS

3	tablespoons butter
¾	cup minced shallots
1	tablespoon chopped fresh thyme
1	cup plus 2 tablespoons medium-grain rice
4	cups canned low-salt chicken broth
¾	cup (packed) grated Fontina cheese
5	ounces soft fresh goat cheese (such as Montrachet), crumbled

Melt butter in heavy large saucepan over medium heat. Add shallots and ½ tablespoon thyme and sauté 5 minutes. Add rice and stir 1 minute. Add broth and bring to boil. Reduce heat and simmer until rice is tender but still firm to bite, stirring occasionally, about 20 minutes. Add both cheeses and remaining thyme and stir until cheeses melt. Season to taste with salt and pepper and serve.

ITALIAN HAZELNUT SHORTBREAD COOKIES

FAVORITE ITALIAN flavors—espresso and hazelnut—come together in these appealing treats. Serve them with the sorbet.

MAKES 4 DOZEN

2	cups all purpose flour
1	cup (packed) golden brown sugar
3	tablespoons cornstarch
1	tablespoon plus 1 teaspoon instant espresso powder
¾	teaspoon salt
1	cup (2 sticks) chilled unsalted butter, cut into ½-inch pieces
1	teaspoon vanilla extract
⅔	cup hazelnuts, toasted, husked, coarsely chopped
2	tablespoons hot water
2	ounces semisweet chocolate, chopped

Preheat oven to 350°F. Blend flour, brown sugar, cornstarch, 1 tablespoon espresso powder and salt in processor. Add butter and vanilla. Using on/off turns, process until mixture resembles coarse meal. Add nuts; blend until finely chopped. Transfer dough to floured work surface. Knead just until dough comes together.

Divide dough in half. Press each half into 9-inch-diameter tart pan with removable bottom. Bake until deep golden brown, about 25 minutes. Transfer shortbread to rack; cool 2 minutes. Remove pan sides. Cut each shortbread round into 24 wedges. Cool completely.

Mix 2 tablespoons hot water and remaining 1 teaspoon espresso powder in small saucepan.

Add chocolate. Stir over medium-low heat until chocolate is smooth. Remove from heat. Cool slightly. Drizzle chocolate mixture over cookies. Let stand until chocolate sets. *(Can be prepared ahead. Store in airtight container at room temperature up to 1 week, or freeze up to 1 month.)*

STRAWBERRY AND ORANGE SORBET

HERE, THE ITALIAN sparkling wine called Asti Spumante is combined with the luscious flavors and bright colors of strawberries and oranges in a refreshing sorbet.

6 SERVINGS

½	cup sugar
¼	cup water
1	10-ounce package frozen sweetened strawberries, thawed
1	cup orange juice
1	cup Asti Spumante or other sparkling wine
	Fresh strawberries

Stir sugar and ¼ cup water in small saucepan over medium-low heat until sugar dissolves. Bring to boil. Transfer to large bowl. Puree strawberries in processor. Add to syrup. Mix in orange juice and sparkling wine. Refrigerate strawberry mixture until well chilled.

Process strawberry mixture in ice cream maker according to manufacturer's instructions. Transfer sorbet to covered container and freeze until ready to serve. *(Can be prepared 4 days ahead.)*

Scoop sorbet into glasses. Top with fresh strawberries and then serve.

BARBECUED TURKEY WITH
MUSTARD-MAPLE GLAZE

SAUTÉED SQUASH MEDLEY

SWEET POTATO HASH

RANCH BISCUITS

SAUVIGNON BLANC OR ICED TEA

STRAWBERRY-RHUBARB CROSTATA

Menu for Eight

SUPPER IN THE COUNTRY

Doesn't matter if you live in the middle of New York City, in a suburb of Chicago or in a town of five thousand on the western plains; if you live in America you can probably relate to the countryside and the time-honored desire for land, open space and a peaceful existence in the lap of nature.

Here's a dinner that will touch the "country" nerve in anyone. It combines the great American passion for barbecuing with turkey, the bird Benjamin Franklin thought was better suited to be the nation's symbol than the bald eagle. The recipe includes the increasingly popular step of "brining" (refrigerating the whole turkey in a salty brine overnight), which produces the moistest turkey possible.

When the turkey comes off the grill, you'll want to let it rest for half an hour. That's your chance to bake the already made ranch biscuit dough (the biscuits cook up golden brown in just 20 minutes), reheat the sweet potato-apple-bacon hash and sauté the colorful mix of zucchini, chayote and yellow squash. Dessert is country-style baking at its best: a free-form crostata filled with rhubarb and strawberries (make it up to eight hours ahead of time) and served with scoops of vanilla ice cream.

Throw a checkered cloth over a picnic table, top it with a bunch of wildflowers, and settle down to enjoy the meal—and the country.

BARBECUED TURKEY WITH MUSTARD-MAPLE GLAZE

TURKEY ON THE grill? Definitely. First the bird is soaked overnight in a brine to improve flavor and ensure moist meat. (Be sure to use a pot large enough to hold both the brine and the turkey.) The smokiness of the turkey is offset beautifully by the tangy, sweet glaze.

8 SERVINGS

TURKEY

- 6 quarts water
- 2 large onions, quartered
- 1 cup coarse salt
- 1 cup chopped fresh ginger
- ¾ cup (packed) golden brown sugar
- 4 large bay leaves
- 12 whole black peppercorns, crushed
- 1 13- to 14-pound turkey, giblets discarded
- 4 cups hickory smoke chips, soaked in water 30 minutes, drained
  Disposable 9 x 6¼ x 1-inch aluminum broiler pans
- 2 large oranges, cut into wedges
- ¼ cup olive oil
- 2 tablespoons oriental sesame oil

GLAZE

- ¾ cup pure maple syrup
- ½ cup dry white wine
- ⅓ cup Dijon mustard
- 2 tablespoons (¼ stick) butter

FOR TURKEY: Combine first 7 ingredients in very large pot. Bring to simmer, stirring until salt and sugar dissolve. Cool brine completely.

Rinse turkey inside and out. Place turkey in brine, pressing to submerge. Refrigerate overnight, turning turkey twice.

IF USING CHARCOAL BARBECUE: Mound charcoal briquettes in barbecue and burn until light gray. Using tongs, carefully divide hot briquettes into 2 piles, 1 pile at each side of barbecue. Sprinkle each pile with generous ½ cup hickory chips. Place empty broiler pan between piles. Position grill at least 6 inches above briquettes. Position vents on barbecue so that chips smoke and briquettes burn but do not flame.

IF USING GAS OR ELECTRIC BARBECUE: Preheat barbecue with all burners on high. Turn off center burner and lower outside burners to medium-low heat. Place generous ½ cup hickory chips in each of 2 broiler pans. Set pans over 2 lit burners. Place empty pan over unlit burner. Position grill at least 6 inches above burners.

Remove turkey from brine; discard brine. Pat turkey dry with paper towels. Place orange wedges in main cavity. Mix olive oil and sesame oil in small bowl. Brush over turkey. Arrange breast side up on grill, centering above empty broiler pan. Cover; cook until thermometer inserted into thickest part of thigh registers 160°F, adding ½ cup hickory chips (and 6 briquettes if using charcoal barbecue) to barbecue every 30 minutes, about 3 hours.

FOR GLAZE: Bring all ingredients to simmer in heavy medium saucepan.

Brush glaze over turkey; cover and cook until thermometer inserted into thickest part of thigh registers 180°F, covering any dark areas of turkey with foil, about 1 hour. Transfer turkey to platter. Tent with foil; let turkey stand 30 minutes before carving and serving.

SAUTÉED SQUASH MEDLEY

Cilantro, garlic and chives accent this zucchini, chayote and yellow squash sauté.

8 SERVINGS

3	tablespoons butter
¾	cup finely chopped white onion
2	teaspoons minced garlic
1½	pounds chayote squash, peeled, pitted, cut crosswise into ¼-inch slices
9	ounces zucchini, cut crosswise into ¼-inch slices
7	ounces yellow crookneck squash, cut crosswise into ¼-inch slices
1½	tablespoons chopped chives
1½	tablespoons chopped fresh cilantro

Melt butter in large pot over medium heat. Add onion and garlic; sauté 2 minutes. Add all squash. Reduce heat to medium-low. Cover; cook until just tender, stirring occasionally, about 25 minutes. Mix in chives and cilantro. Season with salt and pepper and serve.

SWEET POTATO HASH

A savory-sweet side dish to have with the turkey. Make the hash earlier in the day and simply reheat it just before serving.

8 SERVINGS

1	pound bacon, coarsely chopped
2	cups chopped onions
3	pounds red-skinned sweet potatoes (yams), peeled, cut into ½-inch cubes (about 8 cups)
2	pounds Granny Smith apples, peeled, cored, cut into ½-inch cubes (about 5 cups)
2	cups canned low-salt chicken broth
½	cup Frangelico (hazelnut liqueur) or apple juice
2	teaspoons chopped fresh thyme
2	teaspoons chopped fresh rosemary

Sauté half of bacon in each of 2 heavy large skillets over medium-high heat until brown, about 4 minutes. Using slotted spoon, transfer to paper towels. Set bacon aside.

Add half of onions to each skillet; sauté until translucent, about 4 minutes. Add half of potatoes and apples to each skillet; sauté until potatoes begin to soften, about 15 minutes. Add half of broth, liqueur and herbs to each skillet. Boil until liquid evaporates and potatoes are tender, about 15 minutes longer. Stir in bacon. *(Can be prepared 4 hours ahead. Cover skillets; keep at cool room temperature. Rewarm hash over medium heat before continuing.)* Season hash to taste with salt and pepper. Transfer sweet potato hash to serving dish.

RANCH BISCUITS

THE DOUGH FOR these tender biscuits can be made up to a week ahead and frozen until ready to use. Serve the biscuits warm with butter, or, for a touch of sweet flavor, try mixing 1 cup softened butter with ¼ cup maple syrup and 2 tablespoons light molasses.

MAKES 16

4	cups unbleached all purpose flour
2	tablespoons baking powder
4	teaspoons sugar
1	teaspoon salt
12	tablespoons (1½ sticks) chilled unsalted butter, cut into ½-inch pieces
2	cups chilled whipping cream

Lightly butter large baking sheet. Sift first 4 ingredients into large bowl. Add butter; rub in with fingertips until mixture resembles coarse meal. Gradually add cream, stirring with fork to blend. Gather dough into ball. Divide in half.

Knead each dough piece on floured work surface 8 times. Shape each dough piece into rectangle. Roll out each into 8 x 4 x1-inch rectangle. Cut each into eight 2-inch squares. Place on baking sheet, spacing 1½ inches apart. *(Can be made 1 week ahead. Cover and freeze. Thaw 1 hour at room temperature before continuing.)*

Preheat oven to 400°F. Bake biscuits until golden brown and cooked through, about 20 minutes. Serve biscuits warm.

STRAWBERRY-RHUBARB CROSTATA

HAZELNUTS ARE teamed with strawberries and rhubarb in this rustic, country-style tart.

8 SERVINGS

CRUST

1¾	cups all purpose flour
½	cup hazelnuts, toasted, husked
2	tablespoons sugar
1	teaspoon ground cinnamon
¼	teaspoon salt
½	cup (1 stick) plus 3 tablespoons chilled unsalted butter
¼	cup (about) ice water

FILLING

1	large egg beaten with 1 teaspoon whipping cream (for glaze)
⅓	cup (about 1½ ounces) hazelnuts, toasted, husked, chopped

¾ cup plus 1 tablespoon sugar

3½ cups ⅓-inch-thick slices trimmed rhubarb
(1½ pounds untrimmed)

10 ounces strawberries, hulled, thickly sliced

3 tablespoons cornstarch

2 tablespoons strawberry preserves

½ teaspoon ground cinnamon

Vanilla ice cream

FOR CRUST: Blend first 5 ingredients in processor until nuts are finely ground. Add butter; cut in using on/off turns until mixture resembles coarse meal. Mix in enough water to form moist clumps. Gather dough into ball; flatten into disk. Wrap in plastic; chill until firm, about 1 hour. *(Can be made ahead. Keep chilled 1 day or frozen up to 2 weeks. Thaw overnight in refrigerator. Let soften slightly at room temperature before rolling.)*

Preheat oven to 400°F. Place 9-inch-diameter tart pan bottom on baking sheet. Roll out dough on floured work surface to 13-inch round. Transfer to prepared baking sheet, centering atop tart pan bottom.

FOR FILLING: Brush dough with some of egg glaze. Sprinkle hazelnuts over dough. Mix ¾ cup sugar and next 5 ingredients in large bowl. Mound in center of dough, leaving 1½-inch border. Fold dough border over filling, pleating loosely and pinching any cracks to seal. Brush crust with remaining egg glaze. Sprinkle crust with 1 tablespoon sugar.

Bake crostata until crust is brown and filling bubbles, about 55 minutes. Transfer baking sheet to rack and cool tart 15 minutes. Slide metal spatula under edges of crostata to loosen. Transfer to platter. *(Can be prepared 8 hours ahead. Cover loosely; keep at room temperature.)* Serve warm or at room temperature with ice cream.

SERVING THE OUTDOOR MEAL

Sometimes it seems that the hardest thing about eating outdoors is getting the food outdoors. And it's often not something you think about until you've already made a good 25 trips back and forth. The trick is to plan ahead. Let your guests know their help will be much appreciated when it comes time to transport everything from the kitchen to the outdoor table, then begin setting out lots of trays, platters and baskets. Fill them with plates, bowls, glasses, napkins, flatware, serving utensils and condiments. If there is a considerable distance between your kitchen and the table, a wheelbarrow or small wagon can make the job much easier.

When you're feeding a big group outside, it's easiest to serve the meal family style. Fill bowls and other serving pieces in the kitchen, then set them on the table for your guests to pass around, helping themselves. Thick ceramic bowls, platters with faded floral borders, big glass pitchers for lemonade and iced tea, and baskets for bread all add an appealing old-fashioned feel to your table.

Another option is to make serving pieces out of the surplus from your garden or the farmstand. Cucumbers, zucchini and tomatoes can be stuffed with any number of salads. Pattypan squashes can hold salads or dips, and melon halves are perfect bowls for fruit salad or even scoops of sorbet.

SMOKED SALMON ROULADES

MUSHROOM SALAD À LA GRECQUE

CHARDONNAY

BUTTERFLIED LEG OF LAMB WITH
ROASTED TOMATO-OLIVE SAUCE

GREEN BEANS

CITRUS AND GREEN ONION
COUSCOUS

CRUSTY BREAD

CABERNET SAUVIGNON

COFFEE, HAZELNUT AND
RASPBERRY TORTE

Menu for Six

Sit people down beside a lake, a creek, a river or the ocean—water, in a word—and they will happily eat just about anything. But when what's on the plate is as appealing as the food in this elegant menu, the effect of all that beautiful water is only enhanced.

What? You don't have a lake? Don't live near one? Cannot simply conjure one up, David Copperfield-like? Don't worry; water is a state of mind. And that state of mind is relaxed, unhurried, romantic—all of which are more important than any actual body of water. (Of course, if there *is* a lake nearby, you won't have to worry about setting the scene; that shimmering backdrop is all you'll need in the way of decoration.)

The menu begins with a kind of "inside-out" take on the smoked salmon-pumpernickel bread theme. The bread is part of a lively filling that gets rolled up in sliced salmon. A portobello mushroom and fennel salad complements a simple but delicious butterflied leg of lamb, grilled and served with a roasted tomato and olive sauce. Green beans and coucous flecked with green onion complete the plate.

And when you break out the spectacular coffee-hazelnut torte with fresh raspberries, no one will care a whit about water—real, imagined or otherwise. They'll just want to know if there are seconds on dessert.

MUSHROOM SALAD
À LA GRECQUE

THE TECHNIQUE for cooking vegetables in water, oil and vinegar is called à la grecque, or Greek style. Fennel, celery, pearl onions and feta cheese round out the salad.

6 SERVINGS

12	pearl onions
6	tablespoons olive oil
2	tablespoons finely chopped garlic
3	cups water
1¼	cups chopped celery
1	fennel bulb, trimmed, thinly sliced
8	ounces portobello mushrooms, stems trimmed, caps sliced
1	tablespoon balsamic vinegar
1½	teaspoons salt
½	teaspoon black pepper
¼	teaspoon ground coriander
2	tablespoons chopped fresh parsley
1	tablespoon chopped fresh thyme or 1 teaspoon dried
1	bunch watercress
4	ounces feta cheese, crumbled

Blanch onions in saucepan of boiling water 2 minutes. Drain; cool. Peel onions.

Heat oil in heavy large skillet over medium-high heat. Add garlic and sauté 1 minute. Add 3 cups water, celery, fennel and onions; bring to boil. Add mushrooms, vinegar, salt, pepper and coriander. Simmer mushrooms until tender, about 30 minutes. Pour mushroom mixture into strainer set over large bowl. Return strained

SMOKED SALMON
ROULADES

MAKES 32

1	cup plus 2 tablespoons pumpernickel breadcrumbs (from cocktail pumpernickel bread)
¼	cup finely chopped red onion
3	tablespoons chopped fresh Italian parsley
1½	tablespoons olive oil
1	tablespoon fresh lime juice
1	teaspoon minced peeled fresh ginger
¼	teaspoon unsweetened cocoa powder
16	smoked salmon slices (each about 5 inches long and 2¼ inches wide; about 9 ounces total)
	Fresh lime twists

Mix first 7 ingredients in medium bowl to blend. Arrange salmon slices on work surface. Place 1 packed tablespoon filling at 1 short end of each salmon slice. Roll up each salmon slice to enclose filling. Cut each roll crosswise in half. Place cut side up on platter. Sprinkle with pepper. Cover and refrigerate until ready to use, up to 8 hours. Garnish roulades with lime twists.

liquid to same skillet. Boil until reduced to ½ cup, about 12 minutes. Combine mushroom mixture and reduced liquid in large bowl. Mix in parsley and thyme. Refrigerate mushroom mixture at least 2 hours and up to 6 hours.

Arrange watercress around edge of platter. Mound mushroom mixture in center. Sprinkle with cheese and serve.

BUTTERFLIED LEG OF LAMB WITH ROASTED TOMATO-OLIVE SAUCE

ASK YOUR BUTCHER to bone and butterfly the lamb and cut the bone into three-inch pieces (to use in the sauce).

6 SERVINGS

LAMB

½	cup olive oil
3	tablespoons fresh lemon juice
2	tablespoons Dijon mustard
1	tablespoon chopped garlic
1	tablespoon chopped fresh rosemary
1	teaspoon black pepper
1	6-pound leg of lamb, boned, butterflied, trimmed (bones reserved)

SAUCE

20	plum tomatoes (about 3¾ pounds)
10	tablespoons olive oil
1	cup chopped shallots
5	teaspoons minced garlic
⅔	cup chopped Kalamata olives or other brine-cured black olives
1½	tablespoons drained capers
4	teaspoons chopped drained anchovy fillets
1¼	teaspoons chopped fresh rosemary

FOR LAMB: Mix oil, lemon juice, mustard, garlic, rosemary and pepper in large glass baking dish. Add lamb and turn to coat. Chill overnight.

FOR SAUCE: Preheat oven to 400°F. Blanch tomatoes in large pot of boiling salted water for 30 seconds. Using slotted spoon, transfer to bowl of cold water and cool. Peel tomatoes. Cut crosswise in half; squeeze out seeds.

Combine tomatoes and oil in large baking pan. Place reserved lamb bones in another baking pan. Roast tomatoes until beginning to brown in spots; roast bones until golden brown and fat is released, about 50 minutes. Cool.

Remove tomatoes from oil and chop. Pour oil from roasted tomatoes into heavy large skillet. Pour off 2 tablespoons drippings from roasted lamb bones and add to oil in skillet; discard bones. Heat over medium-high heat. Add shallots and garlic and sauté 3 minutes. Add tomatoes and all remaining ingredients and stir until heated through. *(Can be prepared 1 day ahead. Cover and refrigerate. Before serving, rewarm sauce over low heat or bring to room temperature.)*

Prepare barbecue (medium-high heat). Grill lamb to desired doneness, about 12 minutes per side for medium-rare. Slice lamb; arrange on platter. Serve, passing sauce separately.

CITRUS AND GREEN ONION COUSCOUS

A LIGHT SIDE dish for the grilled leg of lamb. Add green beans to the menu, too.

6 SERVINGS

6	cups canned low-salt chicken broth
3	cups couscous (about two 10-ounce packages)
1	cup chopped green onions
1	tablespoon grated orange peel
1	tablespoon grated lemon peel

Bring broth to boil in heavy large saucepan. Stir in couscous. Reduce heat and simmer 2 minutes. Remove from heat. Cover and let stand 15 minutes. Uncover and mix in remaining ingredients. Season to taste with salt and pepper. Transfer to large bowl. *(Can be prepared 2 hours ahead. Cover and keep at room temperature.)* Serve warm or at room temperature.

COFFEE, HAZELNUT AND RASPBERRY TORTE

THIS BEAUTIFUL DESSERT can be prepared up to a day before serving. Coffee flavors both the cake and the frosting, a luscious mix of whipped cream and white chocolate.

8 TO 10 SERVINGS

FILLING

1	cup frozen unsweetened raspberries, thawed, drained
1	cup raspberry jam

FROSTING

2½	cups chilled whipping cream
10	ounces good-quality white chocolate (such as Lindt or Baker's), chopped
3	tablespoons plus 1 teaspoon instant coffee crystals

CAKE

1	cup hazelnuts, toasted, husked
1	cup sifted all purpose flour
1¼	cups sugar
1	teaspoon instant coffee crystals
¼	teaspoon salt
6	large eggs, separated
¼	cup water
1	teaspoon vanilla extract
	Fresh raspberries (optional)

FOR FILLING: Press raspberries through fine sieve into small bowl. Press jam through same sieve into raspberry puree; discard seeds. Stir to blend well. Cover and chill overnight.

FOR FROSTING: Combine ¾ cup cream, white chocolate and coffee crystals in heavy medium saucepan. Stir over low heat just until chocolate melts, coffee dissolves and mixture is smooth. Remove from heat. Let stand until cool and thick, whisking occasionally, about 1½ hours.

Using electric mixer, beat 1¾ cups cream in large bowl until firm peaks form. Fold large spoonful of whipped cream into chocolate mixture to lighten. Fold chocolate mixture into whipped cream in 4 additions. Cover and refrigerate until very firm, about 6 hours. *(Can be prepared 1 day ahead; keep chilled.)*

FOR CAKE: Preheat oven to 350°F. Line three 9-inch-diameter cake pans with 1½-inch-high sides with parchment. Butter and flour parchment. Combine hazelnuts, flour, ¼ cup sugar, instant coffee crystals and salt in processor. Blend until hazelnuts are finely ground.

Using electric mixer, beat yolks and ½ cup sugar in large bowl until very thick, about 5 minutes. Beat in ¼ cup water and vanilla. Stir in flour mixture. Using clean dry beaters, beat egg whites in large bowl until soft peaks form. Gradually add ½ cup sugar, beating until stiff but not dry. Fold into yolk mixture in 3 additions.

Transfer batter to prepared pans. Bake cakes until tester inserted into center comes out clean, about 18 minutes. Cool cakes in pans on racks. Cut around pan sides to loosen cakes. Turn cakes out; peel off parchment.

Place 1 cake on platter and second cake on piece of foil. Spread ⅓ cup filling over each; let stand 20 minutes to set up. Spread 1 cup frosting over each. Lift cake off foil; place atop cake on platter. Top with third cake. Spread remaining frosting decoratively over sides and top of torte. *(Can be prepared 1 day ahead. Cover with cake dome and refrigerate.)*

Garnish torte with fresh berries, if desired. Cut into wedges and serve.

THE PRACTICAL STUFF

A promising alfresco party can be plagued by any number of problems, the most common of which are bad weather and bugs. Always have a backup plan in case of rain, and consider your guests' comfort when picking a site. If the day is very sunny, set up under a shade tree, or use a market umbrella or canopy. Plan for wind: Clamps or clip-on weights (available in kitchen-supply and hardware stores) will keep the tablecloth in place. Or thread the corners of the cloth through heavy napkin rings, then tie knots below the rings. If the party will stretch from afternoon into the evening, you might want to bring out a pile of heavy sweaters, sweatshirts and throws.

Have some bug spray or insect repellent handy, and burn citronella candles. Certain herbs—rosemary, sage and thyme, among them—are natural bug repellents. Keep the food covered, either with dish towels or with mesh domes.

Another consideration is food safety. Again, try to keep the buffet and the table out of direct sunlight. Anything that could spoil should be kept in a bowl set into a larger bowl of ice. If it's not too much trouble, put out only moderate amounts of each dish and keep the rest refrigerated or in a cooler until you need it.

CURRIED BEEF SAMOSAS

CARROT SOUP WITH MINT CREAM

TANDOORI CHICKEN KEBABS
WITH CAULIFLOWER

CUCUMBER RAITA

BASMATI RICE

GOAT CHEESE-ONION NAAN

INDIAN BEER

MANGO TARTLETS WITH LIME CURD

Menu for Eight

No traveler returns from India without a permanent memory of some particularly striking sunset vision: the Taj Mahal, the beaches of Goa, a Himalayan peak, magenta saris against the buff Thar Desert. India is dramatic— more so at sunset. Its food is dramatic too—intensely flavored and vastly varied. Imagine how much fun you can have with an Indian dinner at sunset.

Now, Indian food does have a reputation for being complex, but it doesn't have to be. Take this menu, for example: It features recipes that are simple from start to finish but still taste of the intriguing flavors that make Indian food so exciting.

In India, *samosas,* the savory filled snack pastries, are made painstakingly by hand; here wonton wrappers stand in as a quick alternative to the traditional pastry. A curried carrot soup with mint cream is up next—and it couldn't be easier (make it two days ahead, if you like). Indian tandoori chicken prepared in clay ovens gets adapted to the barbecue here, to be served with fragrant basmati rice, the yogurt and cucumber salad called *raita* and oniony *naan* flatbread.

Finally, in the spirit of adventure, there are lovely individual tartlets that pay homage to India's bright mangoes, adding one more color to this wonderful sunset meal.

CURRIED BEEF SAMOSAS

WONTON WRAPPERS are used for these Indian appetizers instead of traditional pastry dough, making them simple to prepare.

MAKES 32

2	tablespoons vegetable oil
1⅓	cups finely chopped onions
1	pound lean ground beef
2	tablespoons curry powder
1	teaspoon all purpose flour
32	wonton wrappers
1	large egg (beaten to blend)
	Vegetable oil (for deep-frying)
	Purchased mango chutney

Heat 2 tablespoons oil in heavy large skillet over medium-high heat. Add onions and sauté until translucent, about 5 minutes. Add beef and sauté until brown, breaking up clumps with back of spoon, about 5 minutes. Add curry powder and flour and sauté 2 minutes longer. Transfer beef mixture to colander and drain oil. Cool.

Lightly flour baking sheet. Arrange 8 wonton wrappers on work surface. Spoon 1 tablespoon beef mixture in center of each. Brush edges with egg. Fold each wrapper diagonally in half, forming triangle. Press edges together. Transfer to baking sheet. Repeat with remaining wrappers and beef. *(Can be prepared 8 hours ahead. Cover; chill.)*

Add enough vegetable oil to heavy large saucepan to reach depth of 4 inches. Heat to 350°F. Working in batches, fry samosas until golden brown, about 2 minutes per side. Using tongs, transfer samosas to paper towels. Serve samosas with chutney.

CARROT SOUP WITH MINT CREAM

BOTH THE SOUP and the mint-flavored cream can be made ahead of time.

8 SERVINGS

½	cup plain yogurt
2	tablespoons reduced-fat sour cream
2	teaspoons minced fresh mint
4	14½-ounce cans (or more) low-salt chicken broth
2	pounds carrots, peeled, sliced
1⅓	cups sliced shallots
2	teaspoons curry powder
2	teaspoons minced peeled fresh ginger
½	teaspoon sugar

Mix first 3 ingredients in medium bowl. Cover and refrigerate until ready to use.

Bring 4 cans broth, carrots, shallots, curry, ginger and sugar to boil in heavy large saucepan. Reduce heat to low, cover and cook until carrots are tender, about 22 minutes. Working in batches, puree soup in processor. Return puree to saucepan. Thin soup with additional broth, if necessary. *(Can be prepared 2 days ahead. Cover and refrigerate. Rewarm over medium heat, stirring frequently.)* Season with salt. Ladle soup into bowls. Top each with spoonful of mint cream.

TANDOORI CHICKEN KEBABS WITH CAULIFLOWER

THOUGH TRADITIONALLY cooked in a clay oven called a tandoor, this version of the dish turns out every bit as tasty when grilled over charcoal. On the side, have the cooling cucumber-yogurt sauce called *raita*.

8 SERVINGS

2	cups plain low-fat yogurt
½	cup chopped fresh cilantro
¼	cup fresh lemon juice
2	tablespoons grated peeled fresh ginger
2	large garlic cloves, minced
4	teaspoons paprika
2	teaspoons curry powder
1	teaspoon ground cumin
1	teaspoon ground coriander
½	teaspoon cayenne pepper
2	pounds skinless boneless chicken breasts, cut into 1-inch cubes
2	pounds cauliflower, cut into florets
4	medium red bell peppers, cut into 1-inch pieces
16	bamboo skewers, soaked in water 30 minutes
	Cucumber Raita (see recipe at right)

Puree first 10 ingredients in blender or processor. Pour ½ cup yogurt mixture into small bowl, cover and chill. Pour remaining mixture into large bowl; add chicken and toss to coat. Cover and chill at least 1 hour and up to 1 day.

Cook cauliflower in pot of boiling salted water until crisp-tender, about 2 minutes. Drain. Rinse under cold water. Add cauliflower to

½ cup yogurt mixture and toss. Thread red bell peppers, chicken and cauliflower on skewers. *(Can be prepared up to 6 hours ahead. Cover and chill.)*

Prepare barbecue (medium heat). Grill until chicken is cooked through, about 7 minutes per side. Serve with raita.

CUCUMBER RAITA

MAKES ABOUT 2¾ CUPS

2	small cucumbers, peeled, seeded
2	cups plain low-fat yogurt
1	tablespoon chopped fresh mint
¾	teaspoon salt
½	teaspoon ground cumin

Grate cucumber into medium bowl. Mix in remaining ingredients. *(Can be prepared 1 day ahead. Cover and refrigerate.)*

GOAT CHEESE-ONION NAAN

NONTRADITIONAL INGREDIENTS—goat cheese and sweet onions—flavor a traditional Indian flatbread. Bake the bread rounds ahead.

MAKES 4 BREADS

1½	cups unbleached all purpose flour
½	teaspoon baking powder
½	teaspoon salt
½	cup plus 2 tablespoons plain yogurt
1	cup crumbled soft fresh goat cheese
3	tablespoons butter
3½	cups sliced Maui or yellow onions
	Olive oil

Sift first 3 ingredients into bowl. Mix in yogurt and ¼ cup goat cheese. Knead on floured surface until smooth and elastic, about 10 minutes. Form into ball. Return to bowl; cover with plastic. Let rest 2 hours (dough will not rise).

Melt butter in large skillet over medium heat. Add onions; sauté until deep golden, about 25 minutes. Season with salt and pepper. Cool completely. Set aside.

Turn dough out onto floured surface. Divide into 4 pieces. Form each into ball. Roll out each to 8-inch round.

Brush heavy medium skillet with olive oil; heat over medium-high heat. Add 1 dough round and cook until brown spots appear all over bottom, about 5 minutes. Turn bread over and cook until brown spots appear all over second side and bread is cooked through, about 5 minutes. Transfer to large baking sheet. Repeat with remaining dough rounds. *(Can be made 2 hours ahead. Cover onions and bread sepa-rately; let stand at room temperature. Rewarm bread uncovered in 350°F oven about 5 minutes.)*

Preheat broiler. Spread onion mixture atop breads. Sprinkle with remaining ¾ cup goat cheese. Broil breads just until cheese begins to melt, watching closely to avoid burning, about 2 minutes. Cut breads into wedges.

MANGO TARTLETS WITH LIME CURD

MAKES 8

CRUST

	Nonstick vegetable oil spray
2	cups roasted macadamia nuts
1½	cups sweetened shredded coconut
1¼	cups shelled pistachios (about 5 ounces)
½	cup (packed) golden brown sugar
3	large egg whites

LIME CURD

1	cup sugar
¾	cup fresh lime juice
10	large egg yolks
½	cup (1 stick) chilled unsalted butter, cut into pieces
2	mangoes, peeled, pitted, sliced
¼	cup guava jelly or red currant jelly

FOR CRUST: Preheat oven to 350°F. Spray eight 4-inch-diameter tartlet pans with removable bottoms with vegetable oil spray. Combine maca-damia nuts, coconut, pistachios and brown sugar in processor. Process until nuts are finely chopped. Transfer to large bowl. Beat egg whites in another large bowl until soft peaks form. Fold whites into nut mixture in 3 additions (mixture will be thick and sticky). Let stand 10 minutes.

Using plastic wrap as aid, press about ⅓ cup nut mixture onto bottoms and up sides of each prepared pan. Place pans on baking sheet. Bake until crusts are puffed and begin to brown, about 20 minutes. Cool crusts in pans 5 minutes. Using oven mitt, gently remove pan sides; cool crusts completely on rack.

FOR LIME CURD: Whisk sugar, lime juice and yolks in large metal bowl to blend. Set bowl over saucepan of simmering water (do not allow bottom of bowl to touch water); whisk constantly until mixture thickens and candy thermometer registers 180°F, about 9 minutes. Remove bowl from over water. Gradually add chilled butter, whisking until melted and well blended. Press plastic wrap directly on surface of curd. Chill until cold, about 3 hours. *(Crusts and lime curd can be made 1 day ahead. Store crusts in airtight container at room temperature. Keep lime curd chilled.)*

Fill each crust with 5 tablespoons lime curd. Arrange mango slices decoratively atop tartlets. Whisk guava jelly in heavy small saucepan over low heat until melted. Brush over mango slices. Chill at least 3 hours and up to 1 day.

THE OUTDOOR TABLE

Your outdoor parties deserve their own supply closet of table coverings, napkins, casual plates and cups, baskets and serving pieces. Keep it stocked, adding items as you happen to find them over the course of the year (buy cheerful plasticware when it's on sale at the end of pool season, for example), and you'll always be ready to set an attractive outdoor table.

While there are tablecloths galore available in shops, finding a nice oversize one can be difficult. Use overlapping cloths instead, or buy yards of fabric right off the bolt, then just hem the ends. Lengths of canvas or sailcloth look great for a casual party, as do Indian-print bedspreads, rag rugs or brightly colored Mexican blankets. Woven straw mats or sisal panels can create a chic, minimal look. Instead of napkins, try setting out colorful dish towels, bandannas or linen tea towels.

A supply of paper plates and napkins will come in handy for back-yard barbecues and pool parties. A collection of stoneware or pottery plates (mix and match for a unique look) will make for a stylish table on the patio, balcony or deck. Speckled tinware, either new or antique, is ideal for picnics.

MIXED LETTUCE SALAD

GRILLED HALIBUT WITH
LEMON-BASIL VINAIGRETTE

BRAISED POTATOES WITH THYME

SAUTÉED BABY PATTYPAN SQUASH

CHARDONNAY

FRESH PEACH-HAZELNUT TART

Menu for Four

Everyone loves a farmstand: It's where the green onions are greener, the melons sweeter, the peaches drip-down-the-chin juicier. It's also where the sky is bluer, the traffic thinner, the pace slower.

No wonder we like farmstands—and no wonder we like to cook what they sell. When you start with just-picked produce, a memorable meal is practically guaranteed. And since the best, freshest ingredients need no fussing, the cooking is easy too.

A farmstand dinner isn't a particularly overt theme for a party, but a menu like this one—planned with blue sky and green fields in mind—is bound to be infused with freshness, simplicity and great taste. So grab a couple of friends and head for a local farmstand early in the day. Pick up the things you need for this menu (along with some of this, a little of that—who can resist?), then make dinner a joint effort back home.

A bunch of fresh greens, a little blue cheese and a light dressing add up to a wonderful salad. Basil, lemon and capers are all the dressing-up that's required to make a sensational dish of halibut steaks. Braised potatoes sprinkled with thyme, and sautéed pattypan squash add bright color and more fresh flavors to the plates. With glasses of chilled Chardonnay at dinner and a fresh peach and hazelnut tart for dessert (featuring an easy crust of frozen puff pastry), everyone is sure to love this take on the goodness of the farmstand.

MIXED LETTUCE SALAD

Blue cheese flavors this delicious mix of radicchio, curly endive, butter lettuce and arugula.

4 SERVINGS

9	tablespoons extra-virgin olive oil
3	tablespoons fresh lemon juice
2	tablespoons chopped shallot
1	teaspoon grated lemon peel
2	cups bite-size pieces radicchio
2	cups bite-size pieces curly endive
2	cups bite-size pieces butter lettuce
1	cup bite-size pieces arugula
⅓	cup crumbled blue cheese

Whisk first 4 ingredients in medium bowl to blend. Season dressing with salt and pepper.

Place remaining ingredients in large bowl. Toss with enough dressing to coat. Season salad with salt and pepper and serve.

GRILLED HALIBUT WITH LEMON-BASIL VINAIGRETTE

The tangy vinaigrette enlivened with capers and lemon works well with any grilled or baked white fish. This dish can also be served slightly chilled—great for a hot summer night.

4 SERVINGS

2½	tablespoons fresh lemon juice
2	tablespoons olive oil (preferably extra-virgin)
2	garlic cloves, crushed
½	teaspoon grated lemon peel
3	tablespoons thinly sliced fresh basil or 3 teaspoons dried
2	teaspoons drained capers
4	5- to 6-ounce halibut steaks (about ¾ inch thick)

Whisk lemon juice, olive oil, garlic and lemon peel in small bowl to blend. Stir in 2 tablespoons fresh basil and capers. Season vinaigrette with salt and pepper. *(Can be made 1 hour ahead. Let stand at room temperature.)*

Prepare barbecue (medium-high heat) or preheat broiler. Season halibut steaks with salt and pepper. Brush fish with 1 tablespoon vinaigrette, dividing equally. Grill or broil halibut steaks until just cooked through, about 4 minutes per side. Transfer fish to plates. Rewhisk remaining vinaigrette; pour over fish. Garnish fish with remaining 1 tablespoon basil and serve.

FRESH PEACH-HAZELNUT TART

6 SERVINGS

1	cup hazelnuts or almonds, toasted
⅓	cup plus 1 tablespoon sugar
2	egg yolks
4	tablespoons whipping cream
½	teaspoon ground cinnamon
1	frozen puff pastry sheet (half of 17¼-ounce package), thawed
2	pounds fresh peaches (about 8 medium), peeled, pitted, sliced
¼	cup peach or apricot preserves
	Whipped cream

Position rack in center of oven and preheat to 400°F. Finely grind hazelnuts and ⅓ cup sugar in processor. Add 1 egg yolk and 3 tablespoons whipping cream and puree until well blended. Combine remaining egg yolk and 1 tablespoon whipping cream in small bowl. Combine remaining 1 tablespoon sugar and cinnamon in another small bowl. Roll out puff pastry sheet to 10-inch square. Brush lightly with egg glaze. Place on baking sheet. Fold ¾ inch of edges in to form rim. Brush rim with egg glaze. Pierce pastry all over with fork. Spread hazelnut mixture evenly over crust. Arrange peach slices decoratively over filling. Sprinkle with sugar-cinnamon mixture. Bake until fruit is tender and crust is golden, about 30 minutes.

Place preserves in small saucepan and bring to simmer. Brush over warm tart. *(Can be prepared 6 hours ahead. Cover loosely with plastic; keep at cool room temperature.)* Serve warm or at room temperature with whipped cream.

BRAISED POTATOES
WITH THYME

Two FARMSTAND favorites—baby potatoes and fresh herbs—shine in this recipe.

4 SERVINGS

2½	tablespoons olive oil
1½	pounds small red-skinned potatoes, sliced into ¼-inch-thick rounds
1½	tablespoons chopped fresh thyme
2	teaspoons minced garlic
¾	cup (or more) canned low-salt chicken broth

Heat oil in heavy large nonstick skillet over medium heat. Add potatoes, thyme and garlic to skillet. Sprinkle with salt and pepper. Add ¾ cup broth to skillet; bring to boil. Reduce heat to medium-low; cover and simmer until potatoes are tender, turning occasionally and adding more broth if necessary to moisten, about 25 minutes. Transfer potatoes to bowl; serve.

DINNER ON THE PATIO

EGG SALAD WITH ENDIVE SCOOPS

COLD TOMATO-THYME SOUP
WITH GRILLED GARLIC CROUTONS

ORANGE-ROSEMARY CHICKEN

GRILLED-VEGETABLE PASTA SALAD
WITH PARSLEY VINAIGRETTE

WHITE WINE SPRITZERS

LEMON BISCUITS WITH
STRAWBERRY-MAPLE COMPOTE

Menu for Six

Back in the eighteenth and nineteenth centuries, when America's wild western half was being claimed and tamed, vast cattle *ranchos* sprang up from Texas to California. Just as the names of the families that owned these ranches echo today in place-names throughout the region, so too do many of the Spanish words they introduced, like *patio*.

Every rancho had a patio, a shaded square where people gathered to eat and drink, dance, relax and enjoy their slice of the great untrammeled West—much as we do today. The ranchos may have since been subdivided and developed, but the concept of the patio as outdoor dining room lives on in the present.

This menu, with its grill-easy main course, is ideal for a slow-paced evening on the patio. Tomatoes star in a do-ahead first-course soup. Fire up the barbecue to grill the croutons that top servings of soup, then keep it hot for chicken that gets glazed with a blend of wine, mustard, rosemary and orange juice (it was oranges that drew many to California around the turn of the twentieth century) and vegetables that add smoky interest to a pasta salad. For dessert, linger over homemade biscuits topped with ice cream and fresh strawberries sweetened with maple syrup. And know that while the West may have changed, the appeal of starlit dining hasn't.

EGG SALAD WITH ENDIVE SCOOPS

FRESH BASIL updates traditional egg salad, which gets served with endive spears as "dippers" and topped with caviar (if you're so inclined) for a pretty presentation.

6 SERVINGS

6	tablespoons mayonnaise
1	tablespoon Dijon mustard
8	hard-boiled eggs, peeled, chopped
¼	cup finely chopped onion
¼	cup finely chopped celery
¼	cup chopped fresh basil
1	ounce caviar (optional)
24	Belgian endive spears

Mix mayonnaise and mustard in bowl. Mix in chopped eggs, onion, celery and basil. Season with salt and pepper. Cover egg salad with plastic and refrigerate until ready to serve. *(Can be prepared 6 hours ahead; keep refrigerated.)*

Place egg salad on platter. Garnish with caviar. Surround with endive spears.

COLD TOMATO-THYME SOUP WITH GRILLED GARLIC CROUTONS

TOMATO TIME is the best time to put this do-ahead chilled soup on the menu. Thick slices of sourdough are brushed with olive oil, grilled and rubbed with garlic, then cut into cubes for the tasty croutons.

6 SERVINGS

5	tablespoons olive oil (preferably extra-virgin)
2	cups finely chopped onions
¾	cup finely chopped peeled carrots
2½	teaspoons finely chopped garlic
1	bay leaf
3	pounds ripe tomatoes, halved, seeded, chopped (about 5 cups)
3	cups canned low-salt chicken broth
3	tablespoons finely chopped fresh thyme or 1 tablespoon dried
1	cup hickory smoke chips, soaked in water 30 minutes, drained
3	¾-inch-thick slices sourdough bread
1	garlic clove, halved
	Fresh thyme sprigs (optional)

Heat 4 tablespoons oil in heavy large pot over medium heat. Add onions, carrots, finely chopped garlic and bay leaf. Cover; cook until carrots are tender, stirring occasionally, about 10 minutes. Add tomatoes. Cover; cook until tomatoes release juices, about 10 minutes. Uncover; cook until juices evaporate, stirring often, about 20 minutes. Add chicken broth and chopped thyme. Partially cover pot and simmer until mixture is reduced to 6 cups, stirring occasionally, about 10 minutes longer.

Cool soup slightly. Discard bay leaf. Puree half of soup in blender. Stir into soup in pot. Season with salt and pepper. Chill uncovered until cold, then cover. *(Can be prepared 1 day ahead. Keep soup refrigerated.)*

Prepare barbecue (medium heat). Place smoke chips in 8 x 6-inch foil packet with open top. Set packet atop coals about 5 minutes before grilling. Brush remaining 1 tablespoon oil over both sides of bread slices. Grill until lightly browned, 2 minutes per side. Rub garlic over bread. Cut bread into ¾-inch cubes.

Divide cold soup among bowls. Top with croutons. Garnish with thyme sprigs, if desired.

OUTDOOR LIGHTING

Perhaps the greatest appeal of dining *en plein air* is the romance of it all. At night, you can heighten this sense of romance by planning how you light the scene.

♦ CANDLES: These are the obvious choice, and for good reason. Nothing is quite as lovely and evocative as their warm, flickering light. Votive candleholders and hurricane lamps are your best bet, since they'll keep the candles from being snuffed out by the first breeze that comes along. Other candleholders can range from teacups to vases or terra-cotta pots. Hollow out a lemon or small squash. Line up twigs around the outside of a candle-holding jar and tie them on with twine.

♦ LUMINARIAS: A traditional Mexican luminaria is just a small paper bag weighted with sand that holds a sturdy candle (use these on calm nights).

♦ TIKI TORCHES: These can be set into the ground along a path or around the perimeter of the party space; be careful to keep them a bit distant from tables and other decorations.

♦ LANTERNS: Another casual and charming way to light your party, old-fashioned tin lanterns can be found in antique shops and in some home-furnishing shops, while paper ones in different sizes and colors are sold at party-supply stores.

ORANGE-ROSEMARY CHICKEN

IT'S ALMOST AS quick to make the citrus-herb glaze that coats this chicken as it is to open a bottle of barbecue sauce—and the glaze has a far more interesting taste.

6 SERVINGS

1 12-ounce container frozen orange juice from concentrate, thawed

⅓ cup dry white wine

⅓ cup honey-Dijon mustard

2 tablespoons finely chopped fresh rosemary or 2 teaspoons dried

4 teaspoons soy sauce

2 teaspoons hot pepper sauce

1 large garlic clove, chopped

1 cup hickory smoke chips, soaked in water 30 minutes, drained

2 whole chickens (about 7 pounds total), each cut into 8 pieces

Blend first 7 ingredients in processor. Set orange glaze aside. *(Can be prepared 1 day ahead. Cover and refrigerate.)*

Prepare barbecue (medium heat). Place smoke chips in 8 x 6-inch foil packet with open top. Set packet atop coals about 5 minutes before grilling. Sprinkle chicken with salt and pepper. Grill chicken until golden, turning occasionally, about 5 minutes per side. Continue grilling chicken until cooked through, brushing glaze over chicken and turning occasionally, about 25 minutes longer. Transfer to platter.

GRILLED-VEGETABLE PASTA SALAD WITH PARSLEY VINAIGRETTE

FOR EXTRA APPEAL, use tricolor pasta in this fresh-from-the-garden salad.

6 SERVINGS

1 cup coarsely chopped fresh Italian parsley

3 tablespoons red wine vinegar

1 large garlic clove

½ cup plus 2 tablespoons olive oil (preferably extra-virgin)

¾ pound fusilli pasta

1 cup hickory smoke chips, soaked in water 30 minutes, drained

2 large ears fresh corn, husked

2 large zucchini, trimmed, halved lengthwise

1 large red onion, sliced into 3 large rounds

Blend parsley, vinegar and garlic in processor until parsley is finely chopped, scraping down sides of bowl twice. With machine running, gradually add ½ cup olive oil. Season vinaigrette to taste with salt and pepper. *(Can be prepared 1 day ahead. Cover and refrigerate.)*

Cook pasta in large pot of boiling salted water until just tender but still firm to bite, stirring occasionally. Drain pasta. Rinse under cold water and drain again. Transfer to large bowl. Mix in 2 tablespoons vinaigrette.

Prepare barbecue (medium heat). Place hickory smoke chips in 8 x 6-inch foil packet with open top. Set packet atop coals about 5 minutes before grilling.

Brush corn, zucchini and onion slices with remaining 2 tablespoons olive oil. Sprinkle with salt and pepper. Grill vegetables until cooked through and beginning to brown, turning often, about 12 minutes. Cool vegetables slightly. Cut kernels from corncobs. Cut zucchini and onion into ½-inch pieces.

Add corn kernels, zucchini and onion to pasta in large bowl. Mix in enough vinaigrette to coat. Season to taste with salt and pepper. *(Can be prepared 8 hours ahead. Cover and refrigerate. Bring to room temperature before serving.)*

LEMON BISCUITS WITH STRAWBERRY-MAPLE COMPOTE

LEMON-FLAVORED baking powder biscuits get topped with a fresh strawberry compote and vanilla ice cream in this do-ahead recipe.

6 SERVINGS

BISCUITS

1½	cups all purpose flour
5	tablespoons sugar
1½	teaspoons grated lemon peel
1½	teaspoons baking powder
¼	teaspoon baking soda
¼	teaspoon salt
6	tablespoons (¾ stick) chilled unsalted butter, cut into pieces
9	tablespoons chilled whipping cream
2	tablespoons fresh lemon juice

COMPOTE

2	1-pint baskets strawberries, hulled
½	cup pure maple syrup
	Vanilla ice cream

FOR BISCUITS: Preheat oven to 350°F. Mix flour, 3 tablespoons sugar, lemon peel, baking powder, baking soda and salt in processor. Add butter; cut in using on/off turns until mixture resembles coarse meal. Add 8 tablespoons cream and lemon juice and blend just until soft moist dough forms. Drop dough by generous ¼ cupfuls onto heavy large baking sheet, spacing apart and forming total of 6 biscuits. Brush tops with 1 tablespoon cream. Sprinkle with 2 tablespoons sugar. Bake until golden, 25 minutes.

FOR COMPOTE: Using fork, mash half of berries in bowl. Slice remaining berries. Add sliced berries and syrup to mashed berries. *(Biscuits and compote can be made 4 hours ahead. Cool biscuits. Cover and refrigerate compote. Reheat biscuits in 350°F oven 5 minutes.)*

Place biscuits in bowls. Spoon compote over. Top with vanilla ice cream.

Orange-scented Crab Cakes
with Fresh Tomato Relish

Fusilli with Shrimp and
Panéed Chicken

Carrot, Radicchio and
Fennel Salad

Crusty Rolls

Sauvignon Blanc

Frozen Lemon Parfaits with
Chocolate and Fresh Berries

Spice Cookie Thins

Menu for Six

Kids, work, travel: When you're busy with the everyday things, you can go months without seeing your friends. To remedy the situation, resolve to have your two favorite couples over this weekend or next, getting everybody into the kitchen for an hour of catch-up conversation while you all cook, then moving outside to enjoy the fruits of your efforts.

This casual menu, with its southern-inspired dishes, is ideal because the food is simple but special enough to make the evening feel like an occasion. After all, you miss these people and you want to let them know it.

While cooking together is fun, you don't want your friends to feel like they're working for their supper. Take advantage of the do-ahead tips in the recipes to get a jump on the meal, so you can all spend more time talking than chopping. The crab cakes and accompanying tomato relish can both be prepared ahead. The main course is a unique pasta featuring sautéed shrimp and pan-fried batter-coated chicken in a slightly spicy New Orleans-style cream sauce. To go with it, there's a snappy carrot and fennel salad (a good assignment for the noncook in the group).

Make the delicious frozen parfaits and crisp spice cookies ahead of time so that nobody has to leave the table once they've settled in—and the old stories and jokes have begun to fly.

ORANGE-SCENTED CRAB CAKES WITH FRESH TOMATO RELISH

BITE-SIZE CRAB CAKES are topped with a richly flavored tomato relish in this starter.

MAKES ABOUT 20

TOMATO RELISH

2	teaspoons balsamic vinegar
1	teaspoon golden brown sugar
¼	cup chopped shallots
1	cup diced seeded plum tomatoes
1	tablespoon fresh orange juice
¼	teaspoon dried crushed red pepper
1½	tablespoons chopped fresh parsley

CRAB CAKES

4½	tablespoons mayonnaise
1	large egg
1	tablespoon grated orange peel
1	teaspoon Dijon mustard
½	teaspoon salt
¼	teaspoon cayenne pepper
1	pound fresh crabmeat, picked over, drained
1	cup fresh breadcrumbs from French bread
3	tablespoons finely chopped green onion
1	tablespoon chopped fresh parsley
⅓	cup all purpose flour
1	tablespoon (or more) butter
1	tablespoon (or more) vegetable oil

FOR TOMATO RELISH: Whisk vinegar and sugar in medium skillet over medium heat until sugar dissolves. Add shallots; stir just until tender, about 2 minutes. Add tomatoes, orange juice and red pepper; stir until heated through. Remove from heat. Mix in parsley. Season with salt and pepper. *(Can be made 4 hours ahead. Chill; bring to room temperature before using.)*

FOR CRAB CAKES: Blend mayonnaise, egg, orange peel, mustard, salt and cayenne in large bowl. Stir in crabmeat, breadcrumbs, green onion and parsley. Using 2 tablespoons of mixture for each cake, form twenty 2-inch-diameter cakes. Place on baking sheet. Cover; refrigerate 1 hour. *(Can be made 1 day ahead. Keep chilled.)*

Place flour in small bowl. Lightly coat each crab cake with flour. Melt 1 tablespoon butter with 1 tablespoon oil in heavy large skillet over medium heat. Add crab cakes in batches; cook until golden, adding more butter and oil if necessary, about 5 minutes per side. Arrange on platter. Spoon some tomato relish atop each crab cake. Serve immediately.

FUSILLI WITH SHRIMP AND PANÉED CHICKEN

THE TERM *panéed* means "pan-fried" in the New Orleans culinary lexicon.

6 SERVINGS

3	eggs
3	cups fresh breadcrumbs from French bread
½	cup plus 3 tablespoons chopped fresh parsley
1	teaspoon salt
¾	teaspoon black pepper
18	ounces skinless boneless chicken breast halves
6	tablespoons olive oil

¾ pound uncooked large shrimp, peeled, deveined

1 cup dry white wine

1½ cups whipping cream

½ teaspoon cayenne pepper

½ cup freshly grated Parmesan cheese

¾ pound fusilli pasta

Place eggs in shallow bowl and beat to blend. Mix breadcrumbs, ½ cup parsley, 1 teaspoon salt and ¾ teaspoon pepper in another shallow bowl. Dip chicken into eggs, then into crumb mixture, turning to coat completely.

Heat 4½ tablespoons oil in heavy large skillet over medium-high heat. Working in batches, add chicken; sauté until cooked through, about 4 minutes per side. Transfer to plate. Discard oil in skillet; add remaining 1½ tablespoons oil. Add shrimp; sauté over medium-high heat until just cooked through, about 3 minutes. Using slotted spoon, transfer shrimp to plate with chicken. Add wine to skillet; boil until reduced to ¾ cup, about 4 minutes. Add cream; boil until sauce thickens slightly, about 5 minutes. Mix in cayenne and grated Parmesan cheese.

Cut chicken into ½-inch pieces. Return chicken, shrimp and any juices to skillet. Stir over medium heat until heated through.

Meanwhile, cook fusilli in large pot of boiling salted water, stirring occasionally, until just tender but still firm to bite.

Drain pasta. Add to skillet; toss to coat. Season with salt and pepper. Transfer to large bowl. Sprinkle with remaining 3 tablespoons parsley and serve immediately.

CARROT, RADICCHIO AND FENNEL SALAD

6 SERVINGS

1 large carrot, peeled

1 small head Bibb lettuce, torn into bite-size pieces

1 head radicchio, torn into bite-size pieces

1 large fennel bulb, trimmed, cut crosswise into ⅛-inch-thick slices

5 tablespoons extra-virgin olive oil

3 tablespoons fresh lemon juice or red wine vinegar

Using vegetable peeler and working over large bowl, cut carrot into long thin ribbons. Add lettuce, radicchio and fennel. Drizzle olive oil and lemon juice over salad and toss to coat. Season salad to taste with salt and pepper.

FROZEN LEMON PARFAITS WITH CHOCOLATE AND FRESH BERRIES

PARFAIT MEANS "perfect" in French, which is how many view this frozen custard dessert made with egg yolks, sugar, whipped cream, and fresh fruit or a fruit puree. This dessert is shown off to its best advantage served in tall, narrow, footed glasses.

MAKES 6

6	large egg yolks
½	cup fresh lemon juice
½	cup (1 stick) unsalted butter, melted
3½	teaspoons grated lemon peel
2	cups sugar
3	cups chilled whipping cream
3	ounces semisweet chocolate, chopped
2	½-pint baskets raspberries (about 2½ cups)
1	1-pint basket blueberries (about 2½ cups)

Whisk first 4 ingredients and 1¾ cups sugar in medium metal bowl to blend. Set bowl over saucepan of simmering water (do not let bowl touch water) and whisk until candy thermometer registers 180°F, about 8 minutes. Pour lemon mixture into large bowl; chill until cool, whisking occasionally, about 20 minutes.

Beat 2½ cups cream to soft peaks in another large bowl. Gradually add ¼ cup sugar; beat until stiff. Transfer 1¾ cups whipped cream to small bowl; cover and chill. Fold remaining whipped cream into lemon mixture. Cover and freeze until firm, at least 6 hours or overnight.

Bring remaining ½ cup whipping cream to simmer in heavy medium saucepan. Remove from heat. Add chocolate; stir until melted and smooth. Spoon chocolate mixture into bottom of 6 parfait glasses or balloon-shaped wine glasses, dividing equally. Cool. Top with 2 tablespoons each of raspberries and blueberries. Spoon whipped cream over. Top with 2 tablespoons each of raspberries and blueberries. Cover; chill at least 1 hour and up to 4 hours.

Top each dessert with generous spoonful of lemon mixture. Garnish with remaining berries.

SPICE COOKIE THINS

SCENTED WITH lemon juice and grated lemon peel, these crisp cookies can be made up to a week ahead and then stored at room temperature in an airtight container.

MAKES ABOUT 54

2½	cups all purpose flour
1	teaspoon baking powder
1½	cups plus 1 tablespoon sugar
1	cup (2 sticks) unsalted butter, room temperature
2	large eggs
2	teaspoons fresh lemon juice
1½	teaspoons aniseed, crushed
½	teaspoon grated lemon peel
1	tablespoon ground cinnamon

Sift flour and baking powder into medium bowl. Using electric mixer, beat 1½ cups sugar and butter in large bowl until fluffy. Add eggs, lemon juice, aniseed and peel; beat to blend. Stir in dry ingredients. Gather dough into ball; flatten into disk. Wrap in plastic; refrigerate dough until firm, about 2 hours.

Preheat oven to 350°F. Butter 2 large baking sheets. Mix cinnamon and 1 tablespoon sugar in small bowl. Roll out dough on floured surface to ⅛-inch thickness. Using cookie cutter, cut out cookies. Sprinkle cinnamon sugar over. Transfer cookies to sheets. Bake until golden, about 12 minutes. Transfer to racks; cool. *(Can be made 1 week ahead. Store airtight.)*

PERSONAL STYLE

There is no law of decorating that decrees exactly what goes where on the table or what is absolutely necessary at a place setting. Your table should be a reflection of your taste and personality, so look for ways to make your party setting unique and charming.

Sometimes a twist on an expected element, like a centerpiece, can make all the difference. Instead of the usual flower arrangement, experiment with potted plants, including ivy topiaries and miniature roses. Slip them into containers ranging from baskets to ceramic pots. You can also use unorthodox items as centerpieces, everything from pieces of a pottery collection to a kitschy flea-market find, an unusual lantern to mementos from a recent trip.

Place-setting markers, newly popular again, can add a whimsical touch to your party. Use a permanent marker to write your guests' names on leaves, stones, small terra-cotta pots of herbs, or seed packets. Or take Polaroids of the guests as they arrive and prop the pictures up against the wineglasses or lay them on the plates.

Another way to make the table yours, and yours alone, is to mix it up. Conventions aside, mix and match patterns, glasses and silverware patterns according to what pleases you. Look for complementary colors, textures and shapes, working to balance the table as a whole, the way you would when designing a room.

*T*here are lots of ways to impress the family—get a great new job, a big new house or a hot new car. A simpler way is to host a party for the whole gang, a cozy evening of great food to show them how much you care—and what you can do.

Now, feeding twenty people takes a little planning, and this menu gives you a big head start in that department; in fact, virtually everything can be done ahead, which means that when your clan arrives, you'll be there to hear all about Cousin Sally's dance classes and Aunt Sonia's trip to Bermuda, not running around the kitchen. You'll be cool, calm, collected and—most important—part of the party.

The first step in hosting a crowd is to make sure everyone has something to eat and drink. Keep it simple by filling a couple of coolers with beer and sodas and placing bowls of chips and dips in strategic locations. With appetites warmed up, everyone will be ready to dig into the main attraction: chili served in small hollowed-out loaves of sourdough bread.

To go with the chili, try the crowd-pleasing cheddar corn sticks (they can be made the day before) and do-ahead coleslaw. Nor will you be fussing with dessert at the last minute: The pineapple, apricot and cherry pies can be finished up the day before.

With the food completely under control, all that's left is the important business of enjoying those you love.

TWO-BEAN CHILI
IN BREAD BOWLS

FOR A CLEVER presentation, serve the chili in "bread bowls." Start the party with purchased dips and chips (for ease).

20 SERVINGS

2¼	pounds dried Great Northern beans
2¼	pounds dried pinto beans
½	cup olive oil
7	large onions, chopped (about 14 cups)
½	cup chili powder
5	tablespoons tomato paste
3	tablespoons minced garlic
3	tablespoons ground cumin
1½	tablespoons dried oregano
1½	tablespoons dried basil
¾	teaspoon cayenne pepper
14	cups (or more) canned chicken broth or vegetable broth
3	15-ounce cans corn (undrained)
5	6-ounce jars roasted red peppers, drained
3	8-ounce cans tomato sauce
20	8-ounce round sourdough bread loaves or ten 1-pound round sourdough bread loaves
3	pounds Italian sausages
2½	cups chopped fresh cilantro
4	cups grated cheddar cheese
2½	cups chopped red onion
2	cups sour cream

Place Great Northern beans and pinto beans in large pot with enough cold water to cover by at least 3 inches. Let stand overnight.

Drain beans. Divide beans between 2 large pots. Add enough cold water to each pot to cover beans by 3 inches. Simmer until beans are almost tender, stirring occasionally, about 1 hour. Drain. Transfer beans to large bowl.

Heat ¼ cup oil in each pot over medium-high heat. Add half of onions to each pot; sauté until tender, about 15 minutes. Add half of chili powder, tomato paste, garlic, cumin, oregano, basil and cayenne to each pot; stir 1 minute. Divide beans, 14 cups broth, corn with liquid, red peppers and tomato sauce between pots. Bring to boil. Reduce heat to medium; simmer until beans are tender and chili thickens, stirring occasionally, about 1½ hours. Season with salt and pepper. *(Can be made 1 day ahead. Cover and chill. Bring to simmer before serving, thinning with more broth if necessary.)*

If using twenty 8-ounce bread loaves, cut off tops. Using small knife, cut out centers, leaving 1-inch shell. If using ten 1-pound loaves, cut each horizontally in half. Cut off thin slice from rounded end of each half. Cut out center of top and bottom halves, leaving 1-inch shells. Reserve trimmings for another use. *(Can be made 1 day ahead. Cover; let stand at room temperature.)*

Prepare barbecue (medium-high heat). Grill sausages until cooked through, turning frequently, about 15 minutes.

Mix cilantro into chili. Ladle chili into bread bowls. Serve, passing sausages, cheese, onion and sour cream separately.

COLESLAW WITH JICAMA AND PECANS

THIS TWO-CABBAGE slaw gets additional crunch from jicama, carrots and pecans.

20 SERVINGS

2	cups mayonnaise
½	cup chopped chives or green onions
6	tablespoons apple cider vinegar
1½	teaspoons chili powder
1	teaspoon ground cumin
½	teaspoon cayenne pepper
1	large head red cabbage, thinly sliced
1	large head green cabbage, thinly sliced
1	medium jicama, peeled, grated
6	carrots, grated
1½	cups pecans, toasted

Mix first 6 ingredients in medium bowl. Combine cabbages, jicama and carrots in large bowl. Add dressing and toss to coat. *(Can be made 6 hours ahead. Cover; chill.)* Sprinkle with pecans.

PLAY ALONG

Children are told to go outside and play, which may be why, as adults, we all still feel more playful than usual when we're outside. Use this to the party's advantage, planning games and organizing icebreakers that will make the event more enjoyable and memorable for everyone.

For a big, energetic group, start a game of touch football or Wiffle Ball. If a less exerting game would fit better with the guest mix, try croquet, badminton, boccie or horseshoes. And in keeping with the current obsession with all things retro, games like gin rummy, charades and mah-jongg can be a lot of fun, as can the classic board games, including Risk, Clue and Parcheesi.

For a more sophisticated icebreaker, start your party with a wine tasting. Each guest can bring a bottle of wine—perhaps different wineries' versions of the same grape, like Sauvignon Blanc or Pinot Noir, or a variety of whites—and have everyone pick a favorite bottle, rate them or take a guess at their origins (cover the labels first).

Another possibility is to organize your party around a theme. Perhaps you or one of your guests recently visited an interesting destination that could be the impetus for a party, like Mexico, Hawaii, Spain or Morocco. You could plan the menu, attire and decorations accordingly, and everyone will have plenty to talk about during the evening.

JALAPEÑO AND CHEDDAR CHEESE CORN STICKS

THESE ALSO come out very nicely when baked in standard muffin cups.

MAKES 48

5	tablespoons (about) butter, melted
4	cups yellow cornmeal
4	cups all purpose flour
1	cup sugar
¼	cup baking powder
4	teaspoons salt
4	cups whole milk
1⅓	cups vegetable oil
4	large eggs
3	cups grated cheddar cheese (about 10 ounces)
¼	cup finely chopped seeded jalapeño chilies

Preheat oven to 400°F. Brush 24 ¼-cup corn stick molds or ⅓-cup muffin cups with some of butter. Mix cornmeal and next 4 ingredients in large bowl. Whisk milk, oil and eggs in another large bowl to blend; add cheese and chilies. Mix liquids into dry ingredients. Spoon half of batter into molds. Bake until toothpick inserted into center comes out clean, about 15 minutes. Turn out onto racks. Wipe molds clean. Brush with melted butter. Fill and bake with remaining batter as described above. *(Can be made 1 day ahead. Cool. Wrap in foil and let stand at room temperature. Rewarm foil-wrapped corn sticks in 400°F oven for 5 minutes.)* Serve warm.

PINEAPPLE, APRICOT AND CHERRY PIES

HERE'S A COLORFUL and creative pie: Apricots, pineapple and dried cherries come together in a filling that offers a terrific balance of the exotic and the traditional. You can make this recipe as either a two-crust pie or a lattice-topped pie.

MAKES 2 PIES

FILLING

2	16-ounce cans unpeeled apricot halves in heavy syrup, well drained, syrup reserved
2	cups diced dried apricots (about 10 ounces)
1½	cups sugar
½	cup cornstarch
4	tablespoons frozen pineapple juice concentrate, thawed
2	tablespoons fresh lemon juice
8	cups ½-inch pieces fresh peeled cored pineapple
1	cup dried tart cherries
¼	cup (½ stick) unsalted butter

CRUST

4	Easy Pastry Dough disks (see recipe opposite)
2	eggs, beaten to blend (for glaze)

FOR FILLING: Bring reserved apricot syrup and dried apricots to boil in heavy medium saucepan. Remove from heat. Let stand until apricots soften, approximately 10 minutes. Drain apricots; discard syrup.

Stir sugar, cornstarch, pineapple juice and lemon juice in heavy large saucepan until blended and smooth. Mix in pineapple. Let

direction. Tuck ends of strips under crust at edge; press to seal. Crimp edge. Brush lattice and edge with glaze. Repeat with remaining dough disk, filling and glaze.

FOR BAKING: Bake pies until tops are golden and fillings start to bubble, about 45 minutes. Transfer to racks; cool pies completely. *(Can be made 1 day ahead. Let stand at room temperature.)*

EASY PASTRY DOUGH

MAKES ENOUGH FOR 4 CRUSTS

5	cups all purpose flour
1½	cups (3 sticks) chilled unsalted butter, cut into 1-inch pieces
4	tablespoons sugar
1½	teaspoons salt
½	cup frozen vegetable shortening, cut into large pieces
2	large eggs
6	tablespoons (about) ice water

Blend 2½ cups flour, ¾ cup butter, 2 tablespoons sugar and ¾ teaspoon salt in processor 10 seconds. Add ¼ cup shortening; process just until very coarse meal forms. Beat 1 egg with 2 tablespoons water; add to processor. Blend until large moist clumps form, adding more water if dry. Gather dough into ball; divide in half. Flatten each piece into disk. Repeat with remaining 2½ cups flour, ¾ cup butter, 2 tablespoons sugar, ¾ teaspoon salt, ¼ cup vegetable shortening, egg and 2 tablespoons water to form 2 additional dough disks. Wrap in plastic; chill at least 1 hour. *(Can be made ahead. Refrigerate for 2 days or freeze up to 2 weeks. Defrost if necessary, and let dough soften slightly before rolling out.)*

stand until juices form, about 15 minutes. Cook over medium heat until mixture boils and is very thick, stirring often, about 8 minutes. Remove from heat. Mix in cherries, butter and dried apricots. Cool completely. *(Can be prepared 8 hours ahead; let stand at room temperature.)* Gently mix in canned apricots.

FOR BOTTOM CRUST: Position rack in lowest third of oven and preheat to 400°F. Roll out 1 dough disk on floured surface to 13-inch round. Transfer to 9-inch-diameter glass pie dish. Fold overhang under. Repeat with second disk.

FOR TOP CRUST: Roll out third dough disk on floured surface to 13-inch round. Spoon half of filling into crust. Drape crust over filling. Trim overhang to ½ inch. Press crust edges together; fold under. Crimp edge. Brush with glaze. Cut slits in top crust to allow steam to escape. Repeat procedure with remaining dough disk, filling and glaze.

OR FOR LATTICE CRUST: Roll out third dough disk on floured surface to 13-inch round. Cut into ½-inch-wide strips. Brush inside and top edge of crust with glaze. Spoon half of filling into crust. Arrange 7 pastry strips across top of pie, spacing ½ inch apart; brush with glaze. Arrange 7 more strips atop pie in opposite

*N*othing suggests warm-weather outdoor fun like a barbecue. Say the word and everyone's calendar clears. No dressing up, no fussing with delicate china, no sitting with straight backs in formal chairs. The RSVP of choice: *We'll be there.*

Barbecues are about taking it easy, getting comfortable, having fun. It's that simple. But that doesn't mean the menu needs to be limited to hot dogs and burgers (as good as those time-honored stalwarts of the back-yard grill can be), especially since it's just as easy to serve something different, like this collection of Italian-accented dishes for the grill.

The meal begins with garlic bread and sizzling shrimp on skewers. If the guests are divided between two tables, place the skewers on two platters so that they can be passed around. If people are sitting scattered around the yard, have them bring a plate right to the grill.

When the shrimp come off the fire, leave the grill on for the next course: balsamic-marinated steaks. They take less than 15 minutes to grill, just enough time to bring out the do-ahead grilled mushrooms and bell peppers (these taste great at room temperature, so you might as well make them before the party) and toss the pesto-flavored pasta salad.

Dessert, fresh blackberry and nectarine cobbler, tastes like summer itself, especially on the heels of summer's favorite party.

HERB-PARMESAN BREAD

THE FAVORITE RECIPE is enlivened with fresh herbs (most any mix of what's available will work) and grilled, in keeping with the party's MO (though it can also be baked).

16 SERVINGS

¼ cup (½ stick) butter, room temperature

¼ cup chopped fresh herbs

¾ cup olive oil (preferably extra-virgin)

2½ cups grated Parmesan cheese (about 7 ounces)

10 large garlic cloves, minced

2 baguettes, halved crosswise, then lengthwise (8 pieces total), each piece diagonally scored ¾ inch deep at 1½-inch intervals

Blend butter and herbs in processor. Gradually add oil and process until incorporated. Mix in Parmesan cheese. *(Can be made 1 day ahead. Cover and refrigerate. Bring to room temperature before continuing.)* Mix in garlic.

Prepare barbecue (medium-high heat) or preheat oven to 400°F. Spread cheese mixture over cut sides of bread.

If grilling, wrap each piece of bread loosely in foil. Grill in foil, cheese side up, until bread is crusty and golden, about 8 minutes. If baking, place bread cheese side up on baking sheet. Bake until bread is crisp and golden around edges, about 10 minutes. Cut bread into pieces, using score marks as guide. Serve bread warm.

GARLIC GRILLED SHRIMP

A CRUMB COATING adds texture and interest to these easy shrimp skewers. Prepare them ahead and grill just before serving.

16 SERVINGS

4 pounds uncooked medium shrimp, peeled, deveined

½ cup olive oil

2 tablespoons minced garlic

1 cup dried seasoned breadcrumbs

½ cup chopped fresh parsley

32 10- to 12-inch-long wooden skewers, soaked in water 30 minutes

Lemon wedges

Stir shrimp, oil and garlic in large bowl to combine. Add breadcrumbs and parsley and toss until shrimp are evenly coated. Sprinkle shrimp with salt and pepper. Thread shrimp on skewers; place skewers on 2 plates. Cover with plastic wrap and refrigerate up to 3 hours.

Prepare barbecue (medium-high heat). Grill shrimp until just opaque in center and coating begins to brown, about 4 minutes.

Transfer shrimp skewers to platter. Surround with lemon wedges and serve.

TENDERLOIN STEAKS IN BALSAMIC MARINADE

BALSAMIC VINEGAR gives the grilled steaks a deep, rich color and flavor. Marinate the steaks at least six hours and up to one day.

16 SERVINGS

- 1 cup balsamic vinegar
- 1 cup olive oil
- 1 cup chopped shallots
- ¼ cup chopped fresh rosemary
- 16 6- to 7-ounce beef tenderloin steaks (each about 1 inch thick)

Puree vinegar, oil, shallots and rosemary in blender until almost smooth. Divide marinade between two 13 x 9 x 2-inch glass baking dishes. Add steaks, dividing equally; turn to coat with marinade. Cover and refrigerate at least 6 hours and up to 1 day, turning steaks occasionally.

Prepare barbecue (medium-high heat). Remove steaks from marinade; sprinkle with salt and pepper. Grill steaks to desired doneness, about 6 minutes per side for medium-rare.

GET OUT AND GRILL

Those who live to grill know what they like when it comes to barbecues. Some will tell you gas grills can't be beat for convenience and ease of use; others swear by old-fashioned charcoal grills, for the smokier flavor they impart and the fact that they can reach higher temperatures than most gas grills. Neophytes may want to spend several weekends researching the options before making a final decision.

Once the purchase has been made, set up the grill some distance away from your outdoor table and make sure that there's nothing flammable right next to it. Read the directions before you begin playing with fire.

Having mastered the smoking beast, turn your attention to the many accessories available. Pick up an array of long-handled tools, including tongs, spatulas, brushes and forks. Fireproof oven mitts are also a good idea. Grilling baskets are helpful for smaller or more delicate items, like vegetables or fish fillets; similarly, a barbecue "wok" will make quick and tasty work of cut-up vegetables. A spray bottle of water is a good idea to take care of any flare-ups.

Skewers are practically an accessory category by themselves. There are lovely metal ones that look terrific on a serving platter, and wood skewers that you soak beforehand (so that they won't catch fire), then toss at the end of the day. Skewers made from rosemary branches, sugarcane or lemongrass will add delicious flavor to whatever you're cooking.

GRILLED MUSHROOMS AND RED PEPPERS

THIS SATISFYING combination can serve as a side dish or a salad. It tastes great at room temperature so you may want to make it ahead.

16 SERVINGS

1	cup olive oil
½	cup balsamic vinegar
3	pounds portobello mushrooms (about 12 large), stems removed
6	large red bell peppers, halved lengthwise, stemmed, seeded
	Mixed salad greens

Whisk oil and vinegar in medium bowl to blend. Season with salt and pepper. Brush mushrooms and peppers generously with some of dressing.

Prepare barbecue (medium heat). Grill vegetables until tender, turning occasionally, about 6 minutes for mushrooms and 5 minutes for peppers. Transfer to large bowl; cool 15 minutes.

Cut mushrooms and peppers into ½-inch-wide strips; return to bowl. Mix in remaining dressing. Season with salt and pepper. *(Can be made 2 hours ahead. Let stand at room temperature.)*

Line platter with greens. Top with mushrooms and peppers and serve.

FARFALLE WITH PESTO AND TOMATOES

THE IDEAL solution to a bumper crop of basil, the pesto here can be prepared a day ahead.

16 SERVINGS

6	cups (packed) fresh basil leaves (about 12 bunches)
1¼	cups (about) olive oil
⅔	cup pine nuts
6	large garlic cloves, chopped
2½	cups grated Parmesan cheese (about 8 ounces)
3	pounds farfalle (bow-tie) pasta
6	cups chopped seeded plum tomatoes (about 2½ pounds)
	Fresh basil sprigs (optional)

Combine 3 cups basil, ½ cup plus 2 tablespoons olive oil, ⅓ cup pine nuts and 3 garlic cloves in processor. Blend until smooth. Transfer to medium bowl. Repeat with remaining basil leaves, olive oil, pine nuts and garlic. Add to pesto in medium bowl. Mix in 1½ cups cheese. Season with salt and pepper. *(Can be made 1 day ahead. Pour just enough additional olive oil over pesto to cover surface. Cover bowl; chill. Remove top layer of oil before using.)*

Cook pasta in large pot of boiling salted water until just tender but still firm to bite. Drain pasta, reserving 1 cup cooking liquid. Return pasta to same pot. Add 2 cups pesto and reserved 1 cup cooking liquid; toss to blend. Mix in tomatoes. Season with salt and pepper.

Transfer pasta to serving bowls. Sprinkle with remaining 1 cup Parmesan cheese. Garnish with basil sprigs, if desired.

BLACKBERRY AND NECTARINE COBBLER

16 SERVINGS

FRUIT

2	cups sugar
7	tablespoons cornstarch
4	teaspoons grated lemon peel
1½	teaspoons ground cinnamon
6	pounds firm but ripe nectarines, halved, pitted, cut into ½-inch-thick wedges
12	cups fresh blackberries (about ten ½-pint baskets) or frozen, unthawed
2	tablespoons fresh lemon juice
¼	cup (½ stick) unsalted butter, cut into small pieces

TOPPING

4	cups all purpose flour
1	cup plus 2 tablespoons finely chopped crystallized ginger
⅔	cup plus 2 tablespoons sugar
2	tablespoons baking powder
2	teaspoons grated lemon peel
1½	teaspoons salt
12	tablespoons (1½ sticks) chilled unsalted butter, cut into pieces
1¾	cups chilled whipping cream
½	teaspoon ground cinnamon

FOR FRUIT: Preheat oven to 375°F. Butter two 13 x 9 x 2-inch glass baking dishes. Mix first 4 ingredients in 2 large bowls, dividing equally. Add half of nectarines, berries and lemon juice to each bowl; toss to blend. Transfer to prepared dishes. Dot with butter. Bake until mixture begins to bubble, about 30 minutes.

MEANWHILE, PREPARE TOPPING: Mix flour, 1 cup crystallized ginger, ⅔ cup sugar, baking powder, lemon peel and salt in large bowl. Using fingertips, rub in butter until mixture resembles coarse meal. Add cream; stir until dough forms. Turn dough out onto floured surface and knead gently until smooth, about 6 turns. Divide dough in half. Roll out each half to ¾-inch thickness. Using 2¼-inch star cookie cutter or round biscuit cutter, cut out biscuits. Reroll dough scraps; cut out additional biscuits.

Place biscuits atop hot fruit, spacing closely. Mix 2 tablespoons crystallized ginger, 2 tablespoons sugar and ½ teaspoon cinnamon in small bowl; sprinkle over biscuits. Bake cobblers until fruit is tender and biscuits are golden, about 25 minutes. *(Can be prepared up to 6 hours ahead. Cover with foil; keep at room temperature.)* Serve warm or at room temperature.

FRESH SPINACH DIP WITH VEGETABLES

POOLSIDE SANDWICH PLATTER

DILL PICKLES

ORZO WITH EVERYTHING

ICED TEA AND SODAS

CHOCOLATE-DIPPED CHOCOLATE
MALTED ICE CREAM CONES

Menu for Twelve

*I*t's summer, it's hot, and everyone's set to get wet. Sounds like a good time for a pool party, with all the rollicking, splashing, floating, diving, bubbling fun it suggests. The good times start with a simple menu that will keep the host in the swim and please any and all of your chaise-lounging friends—kids and grown-ups alike.

Chips and dip are both quintessential summer eats; they're the right stuff for snacking around the pool. Included in this menu is a fresh spinach dip, made in the processor in minutes. Put some out on the buffet table too, to go with the do-it-yourself sandwich center consisting of assorted luncheon meats, cheeses and breads, plus the obvious go-withs—lettuce and tomatoes—and the less obvious, like the three terrific-tasing spreads offered here. Add a super-easy, do-ahead orzo salad that's loaded with goodies (sun-dried tomatoes, Kalamata olives and pine nuts among them) and let the good times roll.

Later, everyone can rediscover the pleasure of an ice-cream-truck favorite: chocolate-dipped, nut-covered cones filled with chocolate malted ice cream. The homemade ice cream is superb (and can be made up to three days ahead), but if time's short, store-bought chocolate ice cream (or almost any flavor, for that matter) will work just fine.

Splish, splash, everyone.

FRESH SPINACH DIP WITH VEGETABLES

FRESH SPINACH, sautéed with garlic, is pureed with sour cream and green onions to create this delicious dip. Carrot, celery and jicama sticks, radishes, cucumber rounds and sugar snap peas all make good "dippers."

12 SERVINGS

3	teaspoons olive oil
4	teaspoons finely chopped garlic
16	cups (packed) fresh spinach leaves (about 10 ounces)
1	cup chopped green onions
2	cups sour cream
2	teaspoons fresh lemon juice
	Assorted raw vegetables or potato chips

Heat 1½ teaspoons oil in each of 2 large non-stick skillets over medium-high heat. Add garlic, dividing equally; sauté 10 seconds. Add spinach, dividing equally; sauté until wilted and tender, about 2 minutes. Cool spinach.

Working in batches, puree spinach and green onions in processor. Transfer to large bowl. Mix in sour cream and lemon juice. Season with salt and pepper. Cover and refrigerate until chilled. *(Spinach dip can be prepared 1 day ahead; keep refrigerated.)*

Serve dip with vegetables or chips.

POOLSIDE SANDWICH PLATTER

SET OUT A selection of sandwich meats, breads, spreads and go-withs so that guests can mix and match to create their own take on the perfect sandwich. Arrange everything on one very large platter, or divide the ingredients among several smaller platters.

12 SERVINGS

1	pound thinly sliced roast beef
1	pound thinly sliced smoked turkey
1	pound thinly sliced honey-baked ham
1	pound sliced Swiss cheese
1	pound sliced cheddar cheese
1	pound sliced Monterey Jack cheese
8	medium tomatoes, thinly sliced
6	large bunches arugula, stems trimmed

2   heads romaine lettuce

French bread baguette sections,
halved lengthwise

Rye bread slices

Sourdough bread slices

Horseradish Mayonnaise (see recipe below)

Lemon-Thyme Mustard (see recipe at right)

Red Pepper Mayonnaise (see recipe at right)

Arrange meats, cheeses, tomatoes, arugula and romaine on platters. Place bread in baskets. Spoon Horseradish Mayonnaise, Lemon-Thyme Mustard and Red Pepper Mayonnaise into separate bowls. Serve, allowing diners to assemble their own sandwiches.

HORSERADISH MAYONNAISE

MAKES ABOUT ¾ CUP

²⁄₃   cup mayonnaise

¼   cup prepared white horseradish

2   teaspoons chopped fresh rosemary

Whisk mayonnaise, horseradish and rosemary in small bowl to blend. Season with salt and pepper. *(Can be made 2 days ahead. Cover and chill.)*

LEMON-THYME MUSTARD

MAKES ABOUT 1½ CUPS

¾   cup Dijon mustard

½   cup mayonnaise

1   tablespoon fresh lemon juice

1   tablespoon grated lemon peel
(yellow part only)

1   tablespoon minced fresh thyme

Whisk mustard, mayonnaise, lemon juice, lemon peel and thyme in small bowl. Season spread with salt and pepper. *(Can be prepared 2 days ahead. Cover and refrigerate.)*

RED PEPPER MAYONNAISE

MAKES ABOUT 2 CUPS

1   7-ounce jar roasted red peppers, drained

2   garlic cloves

1½   cups mayonnaise

1   teaspoon paprika

Cayenne pepper (to taste)

Puree red peppers and garlic in processor. Transfer to small bowl. Whisk in mayonnaise and paprika. Season with salt and cayenne. *(Can be prepared 2 days ahead. Cover and chill.)*

ORZO WITH EVERYTHING

A SUITABLY NAMED pasta salad that's loaded with flavorful ingredients—sun-dried tomatoes, Kalamata olives, basil and Parmesan.

12 SERVINGS

3	cups orzo (rice-shaped pasta; about 20 ounces)
⅔	cup (packed) chopped drained oil-packed sun-dried tomatoes
10	tablespoons extra-virgin olive oil
½	cup balsamic vinegar
½	cup (packed) chopped Kalamata olives or other brine-cured black olives
2	cups finely chopped radicchio (about 2 small heads)
1	cup pine nuts, toasted
1	cup chopped fresh basil
1	cup freshly grated Parmesan cheese
4	large garlic cloves, minced

Cook orzo in pot of boiling salted water until just tender but still firm to bite. Drain well. Transfer to large bowl. Add sun-dried tomatoes, oil, vinegar and olives and toss to blend. Let stand until cool. *(Can be prepared 6 hours ahead. Cover and refrigerate. Bring orzo mixture to room temperature before continuing.)*

Mix radicchio, pine nuts, basil, Parmesan and garlic into orzo mixture. Season salad to taste with salt and pepper and serve.

CHOCOLATE-DIPPED CHOCOLATE MALTED ICE CREAM CONES

ONE SURE WAY to get the kids out of the pool is to serve up these chocolate-dipped ice cream cones. (If you want the real taste of chocolate malt you'll have to make your own ice cream, but if time is tight, any purchased ice cream will work fine.)

MAKES 12

2	cups finely chopped walnuts (about 8 ounces)
8	ounces semisweet chocolate, chopped
2	tablespoons vegetable oil
12	waffle cones or old-fashioned sugar cones
	Chocolate Malted Ice Cream (see recipe opposite)

Place nuts on large plate. Place chocolate in medium metal bowl. Place bowl over small saucepan of barely simmering water and stir until chocolate melts. Remove bowl from over water. Mix oil into chocolate. Let chocolate stand until cool but still liquid, about 5 minutes. Dip wide end of 1 cone into chocolate, rotating to coat 2 inches of cone and tilting bowl if necessary. Hold cone until chocolate is almost set, about 10 seconds. Immediately roll dipped portion of cone in nuts, pressing gently to adhere. Place cone, dipped side up, in small glass and place in freezer. Repeat with remaining cones; freeze until firm, about 1 hour. *(Can be prepared 2 days ahead. Wrap each in plastic wrap.)*

Using small spoon, gently pack some Chocolate Malted Ice Cream into hollow part of each cone. Top each cone with generous scoop of ice cream. Serve immediately.

CHOCOLATE MALTED ICE CREAM

MAKES ABOUT 1½ QUARTS

- 8 ounces semisweet chocolate, chopped
- 2 cups whipping cream
- 2 cups half and half
- 4 large egg yolks
- ¾ cup sugar
- ¾ cup plain malted milk powder
- 1 tablespoon vanilla extract

Melt chocolate in top of double boiler over simmering water, stirring until melted. Pour into large bowl. Bring cream and half and half to boil in heavy medium saucepan. Whisk yolks and sugar in medium bowl to blend. Gradually whisk hot cream mixture into yolks. Return mixture to saucepan and stir over medium-low heat until custard thickens and leaves path on back of spoon when finger is drawn across, about 5 minutes; do not boil. Gradually whisk custard into chocolate. Whisk in malted milk and vanilla (custard may appear grainy). Press plastic wrap onto surface of custard; refrigerate until well chilled, preferably overnight.

Process custard in ice cream maker according to manufacturer's instructions. Transfer to container; freeze until firm. *(Can be prepared up to 3 days ahead.)*

PARTY FAVORS

We may outgrow birthday parties involving clowns and decorated cakes, but nobody's ever too old for a party favor.

Your guests will always appreciate a memento. Pick out something specific to the occasion: For instance, if you've held a quiet luncheon in your garden, you might want to give everyone a small pot of herbs. An elegant patio dinner could end with guests being handed small glass oil lamps or pretty votive candleholders. At an old-fashioned back-yard picnic, have wooden fans beside each place setting, perhaps with guests' names on them; they'll help beat the heat and serve as nice favors.

Kites are a great way to keep children and adults alike happy, and they're a much appreciated gift. At a pool party or a clambake, have beach balls, silly sunglasses, beach pails and shovels, bubbles, or candy necklaces for the kids, and straw hats for the grown-ups.

For any party that revolves around a particular cuisine, such as Indian or Mexican food, search out objects in import stores that come from those countries. Alternatively, visit specialty foods stores and make gift baskets of spices and ingredients unique to the region. Add a cookbook for a special favor, one they'll remember.

Menu for Fifty

A block party is a great old tradition: It celebrates friendship, it pays tribute to the shared sense of belonging that underscores the notion of neighborhood, and it's a heck of a lot of fun in the bargain. We've got the food; all you need are the folks who will lend a hand.

The planning should be a group effort from the start. Involve your neighbors in setting a date; then enlist their help in assigning tasks, from rounding up supplies and checking on permits to organizing different games and activities.

When it comes to the food, there are a couple of different approaches your group could take. In the menu here, there are nine recipes: two main courses, five side dishes and two desserts. Each dessert yields twenty-five servings; the remaining dishes serve ten. The cooking assignments can be parceled out according to the number of people at the party and the number of families on your block. You can ask people to cook in portions of fifty (multiplying the ten-serving recipes by five). Alternatively, you can organize the food in a less exacting fashion, assuming that not everyone will eat everything on the buffet table and asking people to cook double portions of the side dishes. Just make sure you have plenty of burgers and lots of dessert.

BEEF BURGERS WITH GORGONZOLA

MELTING BLUE CHEESE fills these tasty burgers, which get served on slices of country-style bread with tomatoes and red onion.

10 SERVINGS

3½	pounds lean ground chuck
10	ounces Gorgonzola cheese or other blue cheese
	Vegetable oil
20	½-inch-thick slices country-style white bread
10	large tomato slices
20	thin slices red onion
3	small bunches arugula

Form beef into twenty 3-inch-diameter patties. Form cheese into ten 1½-inch rounds; place cheese rounds atop 10 beef patties. Top each with another beef patty, sealing at edges. Season with pepper. *(Can be prepared 1 day ahead. Place between layers of waxed paper. Cover and chill.)*

Prepare barbecue (medium-high heat) or preheat broiler. Brush barbecue rack with vegetable oil. Grill burgers until charred outside but still juicy, about 3 minutes per side. Grill bread slices until lightly toasted, about 1 minute per side. Place each burger on 1 bread slice. Top with tomato, onion, arugula and another bread slice and serve.

HERBED CHICKEN BURGERS

A CHILI-CRANBERRY sauce makes an interesting condiment to have with these burgers.

10 SERVINGS

3¾	cups dried herb-seasoned stuffing cubes (about 14 ounces)
2½	pounds ground chicken or turkey
1¼	cups finely chopped celery
1¼	cups finely chopped onion
5	large egg yolks
1¼	teaspoons salt
1¼	teaspoons black pepper
1¼	cups bottled chili sauce
1¼	cups canned whole berry cranberry sauce
	Vegetable oil
10	large sesame seed hamburger buns

Grind stuffing in processor until fine crumbs form. Transfer 2½ cups crumbs to large bowl. Mix in chicken, celery, onion, egg yolks, salt and pepper. Form mixture into ten ¾-inch-thick patties. Place remaining crumbs in shallow bowl. Dip patties into crumbs, coating completely. *(Can be prepared 2 hours ahead. Place patties between layers of waxed paper. Cover and refrigerate.)* Mix chili sauce and cranberry sauce in medium bowl to blend.

Prepare barbecue (medium-high heat) or preheat broiler. Brush barbecue rack with oil. Grill chicken burgers until golden brown outside, and cooked through and white inside, about 7 minutes per side. Spread chili-cranberry sauce over bottom half of each bun. Top with burgers and bun tops.

MIXED GREENS WITH FRENCH DRESSING

THIS HOMEMADE French dressing is a reduced-calorie version of the store-bought kind. It can be made up to a week ahead.

MAKES ABOUT 3 CUPS

1	cup ketchup
½	cup cider vinegar
6	tablespoons sugar
⅓	cup vegetable oil
⅓	cup water
¼	cup fresh lemon juice
¼	cup chopped onion
1	teaspoon paprika
1	teaspoon garlic powder
	Cayenne pepper
	Mixed greens

Combine first 9 ingredients in blender. Blend until smooth. Season to taste with cayenne pepper, salt and black pepper. Transfer to medium bowl. *(Can be made 1 week ahead. Cover; chill.)* Serve with mixed greens.

BOSTON BAKED BEANS

THE BEANS NEED to soak in water overnight, so start this recipe at least a day ahead.

10 SERVINGS

1	pound dried pinto beans (2¼ cups)
12	bacon slices (about 8 ounces), cut into ½-inch pieces
8	cups water
1⅓	cups chopped onion
1	cup ketchup
⅓	cup pure maple syrup
¼	cup apple cider vinegar
¼	cup dry mustard
2	tablespoons mild-flavored (light) molasses
2	bay leaves
1½	tablespoons finely chopped garlic
1	teaspoon salt
1	teaspoon black pepper

Place beans in large bowl. Add enough water to cover by 3 inches. Let stand overnight. Drain beans thoroughly; set aside.

Preheat oven to 350°F. Cook bacon in heavy large pot until crisp, about 8 minutes. Add beans and all remaining ingredients to pot. Bring bean mixture to boil.

Transfer pot to oven. Bake uncovered until beans are tender and liquid thickens, stirring occasionally, about 4 hours. *(Can be prepared 1 day ahead. Cover and refrigerate. Bring beans to simmer before serving.)*

PASTA WITH ROASTED VEGETABLES, TOMATOES AND BASIL

GREAT SERVED warm or at room temperature.

10 SERVINGS

	Nonstick vegetable oil spray
3	red bell peppers, cut into ½-inch pieces
1½	medium eggplants, unpeeled, cut into ½-inch pieces
1½	large yellow crookneck squash, cut into ½-inch pieces
2¼	cups ½-inch pieces peeled butternut squash
6	tablespoons olive oil
1½	pounds penne pasta
3	medium tomatoes, cored, seeded, diced
¾	cup chopped fresh basil or 2¼ tablespoons dried
3	tablespoons balsamic vinegar
2	garlic cloves, minced
¾	cup grated Parmesan cheese

Preheat oven to 450°F. Spray large roasting pan with nonstick spray. Combine red bell peppers, eggplant, crookneck squash and butternut squash in prepared pan. Drizzle with 3 tablespoons olive oil; sprinkle with salt and pepper. Toss to coat. Roast until vegetables are tender and beginning to brown, stirring occasionally, approximately 25 minutes.

Meanwhile, cook pasta in large pot of boiling salted water until tender but still firm to bite. Drain; reserve ¾ cup cooking liquid.

Combine pasta, roasted vegetables, tomatoes and basil in large bowl. Add remaining 3 tablespoons oil, vinegar and garlic. Toss to combine.

Season pasta to taste with salt and pepper, adding reserved cooking liquid by tablespoonfuls to moisten, if desired. Mound pasta on platter. Sprinkle with Parmesan and serve. *(Can be made 2 hours ahead. Cover and keep at room temperature.)*

CELERY SEED COLESLAW

THIS PRETTY SLAW with a celery seed and cider vinegar dressing is perfect for a cookout.

10 SERVINGS

12	cups thinly sliced green cabbage (about ¾ large head)
1	cup thinly sliced green onions
¾	cup finely chopped carrots
¾	cup chopped green bell pepper
¾	cup low-fat mayonnaise
3	tablespoons apple cider vinegar
2	teaspoons celery seeds

Combine cabbage, green onions, carrots and bell pepper in large bowl. *(Can be prepared 1 day ahead. Cover and refrigerate.)*

Whisk mayonnaise, apple cider vinegar and celery seeds in medium bowl to blend. Add dressing to cabbage mixture and toss to coat. Season to taste with salt and pepper. *(Can be prepared 3 hours ahead. Cover and refrigerate.)*

NEW-FASHIONED
POTATO SALAD

Zucchini and dill add a fresh twist to the classic, which is a winner served with other summer classics, like the burgers here.

10 SERVINGS

1	cup mayonnaise
¾	cup distilled white vinegar
6	green onions, minced
8	tablespoons chopped fresh dill
½	cup buttermilk
1	teaspoon salt
4	medium zucchini (about 20 ounces), trimmed, sliced into very thin rounds
4½	pounds small white potatoes, peeled, sliced into generous ¼-inch-thick rounds
10	peeled hard-boiled eggs, sliced
2	cups thinly sliced celery

Combine mayonnaise, ¼ cup vinegar, minced green onions, 6 tablespoons dill and buttermilk in medium bowl; whisk to blend. Season to taste with salt and pepper. Cover and chill at least 1 hour and up to 1 day.

Combine remaining ½ cup vinegar, 2 tablespoons dill and 1 teaspoon salt in large bowl; mix in zucchini. Let stand at least 1 hour and up to 3 hours at room temperature, tossing occasionally. Drain thoroughly.

Steam potatoes until just tender, about 12 minutes. Cool to just warm, about 10 minutes. Transfer to 2 large bowls, dividing equally. Add sliced eggs, celery and zucchini. Mix in dressing, dividing equally. Season with salt and pepper. *(Can be prepared 2 hours ahead. Cover salad and let stand at room temperature.)*

COOKING LARGE

Nothing is more neighborly than an all-come, fun and festive block party. It does, however, require good planning and good food. To make your block party—or any other gathering where large quantities of food are involved—a success, follow these helpful hints for multiplying recipes.

◆ Multiply the quantities of ingredients needed before you start the recipe, and write them down. That way you can check your multiplication for accuracy and ensure that you have the correct amounts of everything you'll need.

◆ Let common sense and taste be your guide when it comes to increasing the amounts of ingredients like spices, herbs and cooking fats. Not all items in a recipe need to be doubled or quadrupled just because the rest of the ingredients have been multiplied. For example, when doubling a recipe that calls for sautéing vegetables in oil, double the amount of vegetables but still use only enough oil to coat the bottom of the skillet.

◆ Look for visual tests for doneness instead of cooking times. Depending on whether the food is cooked in batches or in a larger-size pan, a doubled recipe may not require double the cooking time. For that reason, use cues like "bring to a boil," "sauté until tender" and "bake until crisp and golden" in place of precise times.

◆ As a rule, baked goods don't double well. It's better to bake more of an individual item (two cakes instead of one, for example).

CHOCOLATE-TOFFEE TRIFLES

LAYERS OF HOMEMADE chocolate cake crumbs, whipped cream and toffee bits combine in this rich take on the English classic.

25 SERVINGS

3	ounces unsweetened chocolate, finely chopped
2	cups sifted all purpose flour
2	teaspoons baking soda
½	teaspoon salt
3½	cups (packed) golden brown sugar
1	cup (2 sticks) unsalted butter, room temperature
2	large eggs
2	large egg yolks
½	cup buttermilk
1	cup boiling water
2	teaspoons vanilla extract
6	cups chilled whipping cream
3	cups chocolate-covered English toffee bits (four 6-ounce bags)
	Semisweet chocolate shavings

Preheat oven to 375°F. Butter and flour two 9-inch square baking pans with 2-inch-high sides. Melt 3 ounces unsweetened chocolate in top of double boiler set over simmering water, stirring until smooth. Remove from over water. Let cool for 10 minutes.

Sift flour, baking soda and salt into large bowl. Beat brown sugar and butter in another large bowl until blended. Add eggs; beat well. Beat in yolks. Add melted chocolate; beat until blended. Mix in dry ingredients alternately with buttermilk, beginning and ending with dry ingredients. Add 1 cup boiling water and vanilla; stir until blended (batter will be thin).

Pour batter into prepared pans. Bake until tester inserted into center comes out clean, about 35 minutes. Transfer pans to racks and cool completely. *(Can be prepared 1 day ahead. Cover with foil and store at room temperature.)*

Divide cream between 2 large bowls and beat until stiff peaks form. Spoon 1½ cups whipped cream into bottom of each of 2 large glass trifle bowls. Sprinkle each with ½ cup toffee bits. Crumble ⅓ of each cake over toffee. Repeat layering with whipped cream, toffee bits and cake, creating 3 layers of each. Spoon remaining whipped cream over tops, spreading to cover. Cover trifles; refrigerate at least 4 hours. *(Can be prepared 1 day ahead. Keep chilled.)*

Sprinkle trifles with chocolate shavings.

SUMMER FRUIT TRIFLES

A DELICIOUS MIX of cream cheese, sugar, whipping cream and vanilla replaces the custard typically used in a trifle. Nectarines, raspberries and blueberries, along with purchased pound cake, make this a delicious variation.

25 SERVINGS

24	ounces cream cheese, room temperature
1¼	cups sugar
4	cups chilled whipping cream
4	teaspoons vanilla extract
8	nectarines, halved, thinly sliced
4	½-pint baskets raspberries
2	1-pint baskets blueberries
2	teaspoons ground cinnamon
¾	cup apricot jam
6	tablespoons dark rum
3	(about) 12-ounce pound cakes, cut into ½-inch-thick slices
	Mint sprigs (for garnish)

Beat half of cream cheese and ½ cup sugar in large bowl until light. Gradually beat in 2 cups cream. Add 2 teaspoons vanilla; beat until medium-stiff peaks form. Repeat with remaining cream cheese, ½ cup sugar, cream and vanilla. Spoon 1⅓ cups cream cheese mixture into pastry bag fitted with medium star tip and refrigerate. Set remaining mixture aside.

Combine fruit, remaining ¼ cup sugar and cinnamon in another large bowl. Mix jam and rum in medium bowl to blend.

Arrange enough cake slices in bottom of two 3-quart trifle dishes to cover. Brush 3 table-spoons jam mixture over cake in each bowl. Top with 4 cups of fruit, dividing equally. Top with half of cream cheese mixture in bowl, dividing equally. Top with another layer of cake. Brush 3 tablespoons jam mixture over each. Top with 4 cups of fruit, dividing equally, then remaining cream cheese mixture in bowl, dividing equally. Cover each with another layer of cake. Brush tops with remaining jam mixture. Top with remaining fruit, dividing equally. Cover; refrigerate trifles at least 3 hours and up to 8 hours.

Pipe cream cheese mixture in pastry bag atop edges of trifles. Garnish with mint.

SOURCEBOOK

STARTERS

Here's a variety of recipes, from curry-glazed chicken wings to a new take on guacamole (this one made with tomatillos), to get your next outdoor event going—deliciously.

PICKLED VEGETABLES WITH GRAPES AND CHILIES

PICKLED VEGETABLES (pictured opposite), a favorite side dish at barbecues everywhere, are transformed with a few exotic seasonings.

MAKES 2 QUARTS

BRINE

3⅓	cups distilled white vinegar
3⅓	cups white grape juice
12	large fresh dill sprigs
8	small dried red chilies, halved
8	whole star anise
4	3 x ½-inch strips lemon peel
4	large bay leaves
2½	tablespoons whole coriander seeds
2	tablespoons honey
1	tablespoon salt

VEGETABLES AND SEASONINGS

24	white and/or purple pearl onions (about 7 ounces)
24	baby carrots (about 7 ounces), peeled
18	small cauliflower florets
15	baby yellow pattypan squash (about 8 ounces), halved
16	⅓-inch-thick slices from 1 large unpeeled cucumber
1	cup stemmed seedless green grapes
2	1-quart or 1-liter wide-mouth jars
1	large red bell pepper, stemmed, seeded, cut into 1-inch pieces
24	small firm cherry tomatoes (about 8 ounces), stemmed
6	whole star anise
6	bay leaves
6	large fresh dill sprigs
2	large garlic cloves, thinly sliced
2	red or green jalapeño or serrano chilies with stems, halved lengthwise

FOR BRINE: Combine all ingredients in large nonreactive saucepan. Bring to boil over medium-high heat, stirring occasionally. Reduce heat to low and simmer 10 minutes. Strain into bowl; return brine to same pan and set aside.

FOR VEGETABLES AND SEASONINGS: Pour water to depth of 1 inch in medium pot; place vegetable-steamer rack in pot. Bring water to boil. Place onions on rack. Cover pot; steam onions until just tender, about 5 minutes. Using spoon, transfer onions to bowl. Cool and peel onions. Steam carrots until crisp-tender, about 3 minutes; transfer to separate bowl and cool. Steam cauliflower until crisp-tender, about 3 minutes; transfer to separate bowl and cool. Steam squash until crisp-tender, about 2 minutes; transfer to separate bowl and cool. Steam cucumber until crisp-tender, about 2 minutes; transfer to separate bowl and cool.

Place half of grapes in bottom of 1 jar. Arrange half of bell pepper pieces atop grapes. Continue to layer half of each vegetable (including tomatoes) in jar, pressing layers firmly to compact and evenly distributing half of star anise, bay leaves, dill sprigs, garlic slices and chilies among vegetables. Repeat layering with remaining grapes, vegetables and seasonings in second jar. Bring reserved brine to boil. Ladle enough boiling brine into each jar to fill completely. Close jars tightly.

Let pickles stand at room temperature until completely cool, about 3 hours. Chill 2 days. *(Can be made 1 week ahead; keep vegetables refrigerated. Brine may become cloudy.)*

LAMB CARNITAS QUESADILLAS

CARNITAS, WHICH MEANS "little meats" in Spanish, is a Mexican dish of small shredded pieces of pork, eaten with salsa or used as a filling. This version features lamb.

MAKES 6

6	cups water
2½	pounds lamb shanks (about 2 large)
2	onions, halved, sliced
2	large garlic cloves, crushed
1½	tablespoons chili powder
1	tablespoon ground cumin
1½	pounds Fontina cheese or cheddar cheese, grated
12	6- to 7-inch-diameter flour tortillas

Place first 6 ingredients in heavy large pot. Cover partially and simmer until meat is very tender and falling off bone, about 3 hours. Transfer lamb to work surface. Cool slightly. Boil cooking liquid and onions until thickened and reduced to 1⅔ cups, stirring occasionally, about 20 minutes Remove meat from bone. Place in bowl. Discard fat and bones. Stir reduced onion mixture into meat. Season to taste with salt and pepper. *(Can be prepared 2 days ahead. Cover and refrigerate.)*

Preheat oven to 350°F. Divide cheese among 6 tortillas, covering completely. Spread ½ cup lamb mixture evenly over cheese on each. Top lamb with remaining tortillas. Transfer to baking sheet. Bake quesadillas until cheese melts, about 5 minutes. Cut into wedges.

CHICKEN WINGS WITH CURRY-YOGURT GLAZE

YOGURT, CURRY AND cumin flavors combine in this delicious Indian-inspired appetizer. It makes terrific cocktail party fare.

4 SERVINGS

1⅓	cups plain yogurt
1	cup chopped onion
¼	cup plus 2 tablespoons chopped fresh cilantro
4	large garlic cloves, crushed
4	teaspoons ground cumin
4	teaspoons curry powder
1¼	teaspoons ground ginger
2	pounds chicken wings

Combine first 7 ingredients in large bowl. Season to taste with salt and pepper. Set aside ½ cup marinade. Add chicken to remaining marinade, turning to coat well. Cover with plastic; refrigerate 4 hours or overnight.

Preheat oven to 350°F. Transfer chicken to baking sheet. Season with salt. Bake until tender and crusty, turning and basting with reserved marinade, about 1 hour.

BRUSCHETTA WITH WHITE BEANS, OLIVES AND TOMATOES

IF YOU'RE SHORT on time, canned white beans will make a fine substitute for the dried in this sophisticated appetizer (pictured below). You don't need to soak or cook them.

MAKES ABOUT 20

1	cup dried Great Northern white beans
3	plum tomatoes, seeded, chopped
¼	cup chopped pitted Kalamata olives or other brine-cured black olives
6	tablespoons olive oil
¼	cup chopped fresh basil
1	tablespoon minced garlic
1	French bread baguette, cut into ⅓-inch-thick rounds
5	to 6 ounces soft fresh goat cheese (such as Montrachet), room temperature

Place beans in large saucepan. Add enough cold water to cover by 3 inches and bring to boil. Cover and remove from heat. Let stand 1 hour.

Drain beans; return to pot. Add enough cold water to cover by 3 inches and bring to boil. Reduce heat and simmer until tender, stirring occasionally, about 1 hour 10 minutes. Drain and cool. Transfer 1½ cups beans to medium bowl (reserve remainder for another use). Mix in tomatoes, olives, 4 tablespoons oil, basil and garlic. Season with salt and pepper. *(Can be prepared 1 day ahead. Cover and refrigerate. Bring to room temperature before using.)*

Preheat broiler. Place bread slices on baking sheet. Brush with 2 tablespoons olive oil. Broil bread until golden brown, about 1 minute. Spread cheese over. Top with white bean mixture.

ARTICHOKE CROSTINI
WITH BRIE

MAKES 24

- 2 6-ounce jars marinated artichoke hearts, drained, liquid reserved
- 6 large basil leaves
- 1 large garlic clove
- 1 French bread baguette (about 8 ounces), cut into ½-inch-thick slices
- 8 ounces chilled Brie
- 1 teaspoon dried crushed red pepper

Combine first 3 ingredients in processor and finely chop. Season to taste with salt and pepper. *(Can be prepared 2 days ahead. Cover and chill.)*

Preheat broiler. Brush bread with reserved artichoke marinade. Arrange on baking sheet and broil until golden brown. Mound 2 teaspoons artichoke mixture on bread. Thinly slice Brie. Top artichoke with Brie, covering completely. Broil until cheese bubbles. Sprinkle with crushed red pepper and serve.

HERBED FETA SPREAD

MAKES ABOUT 1½ CUPS

- ¾ cup (1½ sticks) chilled unsalted butter, cut into pieces
- 6 ounces feta cheese
- 3 green onions, chopped
- 1 tablespoon minced fresh rosemary
- 2 teaspoons grated lemon peel

Mix all ingredients in processor until smooth. Transfer to small bowl. Season to taste with salt and pepper. *(Spread can be prepared 2 days ahead. Cover and refrigerate. Let stand 1 hour at room temperature before serving.)*

HUMMUS WITH YOGURT
AND LEMON

IN THIS MODIFIED version of the Middle Eastern garbanzo bean dip, yogurt replaces some of the high-fat tahini (sesame seed paste). The dip is great with fresh vegetables or toasted pita bread wedges.

MAKES ABOUT 1½ CUPS

- 2 large garlic cloves
- 1 15-ounce can garbanzo beans (chickpeas), drained
- 2 tablespoons plain nonfat yogurt
- 2 tablespoons tahini (sesame seed paste)*
- 2 tablespoons fresh lemon juice
- 1 teaspoon ground cumin

Mince garlic in processor. Add remaining ingredients; blend until coarse puree forms, occasionally scraping down sides of work bowl. Season hummus to taste with salt and pepper. Transfer to small bowl. *(Can be made 3 days ahead. Cover and chill. Bring to room temperature before serving.)*

Tahini is available at natural foods stores and in some supermarkets.

PROSCIUTTO-WRAPPED SHRIMP WITH GARLIC DIPPING SAUCE

THESE SHRIMP SKEWERS taste as good at room temperature as they do hot off the grill.

6 SERVINGS

18	thin slices prosciutto
18	fresh basil leaves
18	extra-large shrimp, peeled, deveined
18	bamboo skewers, soaked in water 30 minutes
1/3	cup red wine vinegar
2	tablespoons Dijon mustard
1	tablespoon chopped garlic
1	cup olive oil

Place 1 prosciutto slice on work surface, short end parallel to edge. Place 1 basil leaf at 1 short end of prosciutto slice. Place 1 shrimp atop basil leaf. Roll up shrimp in prosciutto. Thread shrimp on skewer. Repeat with remaining prosciutto, basil, shrimp and skewers. *(Can be made 1 day ahead. Wrap tightly in plastic and chill.)*

Prepare barbecue (medium-high heat) or preheat broiler. Combine vinegar, mustard and garlic in blender. Gradually add oil; blend well. Transfer dipping sauce to small bowl. Season sauce with salt and pepper.

Grill wrapped shrimp until opaque in center, turning frequently, about 6 minutes. Transfer to platter. Serve shrimp skewers hot or at room temperature with sauce.

TOMATILLO-AVOCADO DIP WITH CHIPS

THIS EASY-TO-MAKE, do-ahead dip is also nice as a topping for burritos and enchiladas.

MAKES ABOUT 2¾ CUPS

1	pound tomatillos,* husked
1	avocado, pitted, peeled
1	cup loosely packed fresh cilantro leaves
1/3	cup sour cream
5	garlic cloves
3	tablespoons fresh lime juice
1½	medium jalapeño chilies, stemmed, seeded, chopped
	Tortilla chips

Cook tomatillos in large pot of boiling water until soft but still whole, about 3 minutes. Drain. Place tomatillos in large bowl and refrigerate until cold, about 1 hour.

Place tomatillos in blender. Add next 6 ingredients. Blend until smooth. Transfer dip to bowl. Cover with plastic and refrigerate until cold. *(Dip can be prepared 6 hours ahead.)* Serve tomatillo dip with chips.

* Tomatillos, green, tomato-like vegetables with paper-thin husks, are available at Latin American markets, specialty foods stores and some supermarkets.

MARINATED OLIVES, RED BELL PEPPER, ARTICHOKE HEARTS AND MUSHROOMS

SERVE THESE MARINATED vegetables with sliced assorted cold cuts and crusty bread.

6 SERVINGS

½ cup olive oil

3 tablespoons red wine vinegar

2 tablespoons chopped fresh basil

1 tablespoon chopped fresh Italian parsley

1½ teaspoons minced garlic

1 teaspoon whole grain Dijon mustard

1 9-ounce package frozen artichoke hearts, thawed, drained well, halved lengthwise

1 large bell pepper, cut into matchstick-size strips

4 ounces small button mushrooms, trimmed, quartered

1 small onion, thinly sliced (about ⅓ cup)

¾ cup pitted Kalamata olives or other brine-cured black olives, quartered lengthwise

Whisk first 6 ingredients in large bowl to blend. Add vegetables and olives. Toss to coat. Season with salt and pepper. Cover and refrigerate at least 2 hours, stirring occasionally. *(Can be made 2 days ahead. Keep chilled. Let stand at room temperature 30 minutes before serving.)*

Transfer mixture to bowl and serve.

SMOKED SALMON PIZZA WITH RED ONION AND DILL

RED ONION, CAPERS and fresh dill make nice toppings. Serve the pizza with lemon wedges.

6 SERVINGS

1 10-ounce purchased fully baked pizza crust

4 ounces cream cheese, room temperature

¼ cup minced red onion

1 tablespoon chopped fresh dill

2 teaspoons grated lemon peel

1 teaspoon prepared white horseradish

4 to 6 ounces thinly sliced smoked salmon

Preheat oven to 450°F. Place pizza crust on baking sheet. Bake until crisp at edges, about 13 minutes. Transfer to rack; cool slightly.

Blend cream cheese with next 4 ingredients. Season with salt and pepper.

Spread cheese topping over crust, leaving 1-inch border. Top with salmon. Slice pizza and transfer to platter. Serve immediately.

LAYERED BEAN, GUACAMOLE AND SALSA DIP

HERE'S A CROWD pleaser that can be completed the day before your get-together.

8 SERVINGS

1½	16-ounce cans refried beans with bacon
1¾	teaspoons chili powder
2	cups purchased guacamole
⅓	cup purchased tomatillo salsa
1	teaspoon minced garlic
2	cups grated cheddar cheese (about 8 ounces)
2	14½-ounce cans diced tomatoes with jalapeños, well drained
¾	cup chopped green onions
1½	cups sour cream
⅔	cup chopped fresh cilantro
1	3.8-ounce can sliced black olives, drained
	Tortilla chips

Mix beans and chili powder in medium bowl to blend. Mix guacamole, tomatillo salsa and garlic in another medium bowl.

Spread half of bean mixture in bottom of 8- to 10-cup glass bowl. Sprinkle with 1 cup cheese. Spread guacamole over. Spoon half of drained tomatoes over. Sprinkle with green onions. Spread remaining bean mixture over. Stir sour cream to loosen. Spread over bean mixture, covering completely. Arrange cilantro, remaining cheese, olives and remaining drained tomatoes in concentric circles atop sour cream. Cover; refrigerate at least 2 hours. *(Dip can be assembled 1 day ahead. Cover tightly with plastic wrap and keep refrigerated.)* Serve dip with chips.

SOUTH OF THE BORDER BLACK BEAN SOUP

4 SERVINGS

2	teaspoons olive oil
1	cup finely chopped onion
4	garlic cloves, minced
2	teaspoons ground cumin
1	teaspoon dried oregano
¼	teaspoon dried crushed red pepper
1	15-ounce can black beans, drained
1	15-ounce can golden hominy, drained
1	14½-ounce can diced tomatoes in juice
1	14½-ounce can beef broth
1	bay leaf
2	tablespoons (or more) chopped fresh cilantro
	Sour cream (optional)

Heat oil in heavy large saucepan over medium heat. Add onion, garlic, cumin, oregano and crushed red pepper and sauté 5 minutes. Add beans, hominy, tomatoes with juices, broth and

bay leaf and bring to boil. Reduce heat and simmer 15 minutes. *(Can be prepared 2 days ahead. Cover and refrigerate. Reheat, stirring often, over medium-high heat.)* Mix in 2 tablespoons cilantro. Ladle soup into bowls. Top with sour cream, if desired. Sprinkle with cilantro.

CHILLED RED PEPPER AND LEEK SOUP

THIS SOOTHING SOUP (pictured opposite) has a nice tang from the buttermilk. To make the garnish, thinly slice a whole bell pepper, then remove the core from each "ring."

4 TO 6 SERVINGS

¼	cup (½ stick) butter
1¼	pounds red bell peppers, coarsely chopped
2	cups sliced leeks (white and pale green parts only)
1½	cups canned low-salt chicken broth
1½	cups chilled buttermilk
	Red bell pepper rings
	Chopped chives or green onion tops

Melt butter in heavy large saucepan over medium-high heat. Add chopped bell peppers and leeks and sauté until tender, about 18 minutes. Add broth and bring to boil. Reduce heat, cover and simmer until vegetables are very tender, about 15 minutes. Puree soup in blender in batches. Refrigerate until cool, 30 minutes.

Mix buttermilk into soup. Season with salt and pepper. Refrigerate soup until very cold, at least 3 hours and up to 1 day.

Ladle soup into bowls. Garnish with bell pepper rings and chives and serve.

ICE IDEAS

At warm-weather outdoor parties, ice is a necessity to keep things cold. But you don't have to settle for an ordinary bag of cubes from the local convenience store; there are lots of other ice options out there.

Look for tray molds that make ice in the shape of hearts, circles, stars and triangles. Decorated ice cubes add a lovely touch to clear drinks. Fill ice cube trays halfway with water, freeze, then dip small flowers or pieces of fruit in water and lay them in the trays. Freeze again, fill the trays with water, and freeze until the cubes are firm. Kiwi slices, berries, mint leaves, lemon slices and even sliced olives all work well. Flavored ice cubes (make them from fresh juices, coffee, lemonade, tea or sodas) can complement different drinks too. Or slice some lemons, freeze the slices in a single layer, then add them to cocktails, iced tea or sparkling mineral water.

For a dramatic centerpiece, place a bottle of wine, vodka or gin in an empty milk carton, fill the carton with water, then add flowers, berries or lemon slices to the water and stick the whole getup in the freezer. Once the water has frozen, peel away the cardboard and set the "ice bucket" on a tray or platter with flowers or vines around the base. (You may need to trickle hot water around the bottle or use a long knife to work it out of the ice.)

MAIN COURSES

Chicken, steaks, ribs, shrimp and more take to the grill in this collection of recipes for alfresco parties; cooling salads and other quick-cooking entrées round out the mix.

GREEK CHICKEN ON POTATO "CROUTONS"

OLIVE-STUFFED CHICKEN breasts are served on grilled slices of potato with a fresh tomato-and-feta relish on the side.

4 SERVINGS

1	pound plum tomatoes, seeded, coarsely chopped
½	pound feta cheese, diced
12	Kalamata olives or other brine-cured black olives, pitted, coarsely chopped
2	tablespoons fresh lemon juice
2	tablespoons extra-virgin olive oil
2	tablespoons ouzo or other anise-flavored liqueur (optional)
4	large boneless chicken breast halves with skin
3	tablespoons olivada*
	Additional extra-virgin olive oil
	Additional fresh lemon juice
2	extra-large russet potatoes, boiled, cooled, peeled
	Fresh watercress (optional)
	Lemon wedges

Combine first 6 ingredients in medium bowl. Season to taste with salt and pepper. *(Can be prepared 1 day ahead. Cover and chill. Let stand at room temperature 1 hour before continuing.)*

Loosen skin of each chicken breast along 1 side. Spread ¼ of olivada evenly under skin and over meat of each. Skewer skin closed. Brush chicken with olive oil. Season chicken breasts with salt, pepper and fresh lemon juice.

Cut four ½-inch-thick lengthwise slices from potatoes. (Reserve remainder of potato for another use.) Brush potato slices with olive oil; season with salt, pepper and fresh lemon juice.

Prepare barbecue (medium-high heat). Grill chicken skin side up, 5 minutes. Turn over and grill until skin is crisp and brown and chicken is cooked through, about 3 minutes.

Grill potato slices alongside chicken until brown and crisp, turning once, 8 minutes.

Arrange potato slices on platter. Place 1 chicken breast on each. Spoon tomato relish alongside. Garnish chicken with watercress and lemon wedges and serve.

*An olive spread, sometimes called black olive cream, available at Italian markets and specialty foods stores. If unavailable, use pureed pitted Kalamata olives or other brine-cured black olives.

CHICKEN SALAD WITH LENTILS AND PEAS

NOT YOUR TRADITIONAL chicken salad. This one (pictured at right) boasts lentils, cauliflower, cucumber and Asian pears.

4 SERVINGS

3	cups water
⅔	cup dried lentils
3	tablespoons fresh lemon juice
3	tablespoons plus 1 teaspoon olive oil
2	large skinless boneless chicken breast halves
2	teaspoons (generous) curry powder
⅔	cup canned low-salt chicken broth
1	cup cauliflower florets
¾	cup fresh or frozen peas
2	small tomatoes, seeded, diced
1¼	cups diced English hothouse cucumber
2	green onions, sliced
3	tablespoons sour cream
2	tablespoons chopped fresh mint
2	large bunches watercress, trimmed
1	Asian pear* or Bartlett pear, peeled, cored, diced
1	large tomato, cut into wedges
	Fresh mint sprigs

Bring 3 cups water and lentils to boil in heavy medium saucepan. Reduce heat to medium-low, cover and simmer until lentils are tender but still retain shape, 20 minutes. Drain well. Transfer lentils to large bowl. Mix in 1 tablespoon lemon juice and 1 tablespoon oil. Cover and chill.

Rub chicken breasts on both sides with curry powder. Season with salt and pepper. Heat 1 teaspoon olive oil in heavy large skillet over medium-high heat. Add chicken breasts to skillet; cook until golden brown and cooked through, about 5 minutes per side. Transfer chicken to plate; refrigerate until well chilled.

Add chicken broth to same skillet and bring to boil. Add cauliflower and peas and cook over high heat until vegetables are crisp-tender and most of liquid has evaporated, about 5 minutes. Add vegetable mixture to lentils.

Cut chicken into ½-inch cubes and add to lentils along with any accumulated juices. Mix in diced tomatoes, cucumber, green onions, sour cream and chopped mint. Season salad to taste with salt and pepper. Cover and refrigerate until well chilled, about 2 hours. (*Salad can be prepared 1 day ahead. Keep refrigerated.*)

Toss watercress with remaining 2 tablespoons lemon juice and 2 tablespoons oil. Season to taste with salt and pepper. Mix pear into chicken salad. Mound chicken salad in center of 4 plates. Surround with watercress. Garnish with tomato and mint sprigs.

*Also called Chinese pear and apple pear. Available in the produce section of many supermarkets.

CHICKEN THIGHS WITH ONION-THYME RELISH

HERE, BONELESS THIGHS are stuffed under the skin with a mix of onions and goat cheese.

6 SERVINGS

3	tablespoons olive oil
1	pound onions, thinly sliced
1	teaspoon dried thyme
1	tablespoon balsamic vinegar
½	teaspoon sugar
6	boneless chicken thighs
6	ounces goat cheese
	Fresh thyme sprigs

Heat oil in heavy medium skillet over medium-low heat. Add onions and thyme and cook until golden brown, stirring frequently, 35 minutes. Mix in vinegar and sugar. Season with salt and pepper. *(Can be made 1 day ahead. Cover; chill.)*

Loosen skin of 1 thigh. Season with salt and pepper. Press ⅙ of onion relish onto thigh under skin. Crumble 1 ounce goat cheese and press over relish. Stretch skin over stuffing and secure with small metal skewer. Repeat with remaining thighs, relish and cheese. *(Can be prepared 1 day ahead. Cover and refrigerate.)*

Prepare barbecue (medium-high heat). Grill thighs, skin side up, until chicken is golden brown and just cooked through, about 8 minutes. Turn and grill skin side down until skin is golden brown, about 2 minutes. Using pliers, remove metal skewers.

Arrange chicken on platter. Garnish with fresh thyme and serve.

GRILLED CHICKEN SALAD

2 SERVINGS

5	teaspoons Dijon mustard
4	teaspoons minced fresh rosemary
3	garlic cloves, pressed
2	boneless chicken breast halves with skin
1	tablespoon plus ½ cup olive oil
3	tablespoons fresh lemon juice
2	teaspoons coarse-grained mustard
2	teaspoons minced shallot
6	shiitake mushrooms, stemmed
4	cups mixed greens
8	asparagus spears, trimmed, blanched
1	tomato, peeled, seeded, chopped

Mix 1 teaspoon Dijon mustard, 2 teaspoons rosemary and garlic in small bowl. Run fingertips between chicken skin and meat to loosen. Rub mustard mixture over and under skin. Drizzle 1 tablespoon oil over chicken. Cover and refrigerate at least 2 hours or overnight.

Whisk remaining 4 teaspoons Dijon mustard, remaining 2 teaspoons rosemary, lemon juice, coarse mustard and shallot in small bowl. Whisk in remaining ½ cup oil. *(Can be prepared 1 day ahead. Cover and refrigerate.)*

Prepare barbecue (medium-high heat). Season chicken with salt and pepper. Grill until cooked through, turning occasionally, about 20 minutes. Transfer to cutting board; tent with foil. Toss mushrooms with 1 tablespoon dressing. Grill mushrooms until soft, turning once, about 3 minutes. Toss greens with enough dressing to coat. Divide mixed greens between plates. Slice chicken crosswise; fan atop greens. Spoon more dressing over. Garnish with mushrooms, asparagus and tomato and serve.

DEVILED FRIED CHICKEN

THIS RECIPE (pictured below) gets its name from the peppery-hot seasonings in the crust. Begin preparing it one day ahead.

4 SERVINGS

2	cups buttermilk
¼	cup Dijon mustard
2	tablespoons onion powder with green onion and parsley
5	teaspoons salt
4	teaspoons dry mustard
4	teaspoons cayenne pepper
2½	teaspoons black pepper
8	pieces cut-up chicken, skinned (except wings)
3	cups all purpose flour
1	tablespoon baking powder
1	tablespoon garlic powder
5	cups (or more) peanut oil (for frying)

In 1-gallon resealable plastic bag, combine buttermilk, Dijon mustard, 1 tablespoon onion powder, 1 teaspoon salt, 1 teaspoon dry mustard, 1 teaspoon cayenne pepper and 1 teaspoon black pepper. Holding top closed, knead bag to blend marinade ingredients. Add chicken. Seal bag, eliminating most air. Turn bag to coat chicken evenly. Refrigerate at least 1 day and up to 3 days, turning bag occasionally.

Whisk flour, baking powder, garlic powder, remaining 1 tablespoon onion powder, 4 teaspoons salt, 3 teaspoons dry mustard, 3 teaspoons cayenne and 1½ teaspoons black pepper in 13 x 9 x 2-inch glass dish. With marinade still clinging to chicken pieces (do not shake off excess), add chicken to flour mixture; turn to coat thickly. Let chicken stand in flour mixture 1 hour, turning chicken occasionally to recoat with flour mixture as needed.

Pour oil to depth of 1¼ inches into deep 10- to 11-inch-diameter skillet or pot. Attach deep-fry thermometer. Heat oil over medium-high heat to 350°F. Shake off excess coating from 4 pieces of chicken; add chicken, skinned side down, to oil. Reduce heat to medium-low and fry 5 minutes, adjusting heat occasionally to maintain temperature between 280°F and 300°F (oil should bubble constantly around chicken). Using 2 wooden spoons, turn chicken over. Fry 7 minutes. Turn chicken over again and fry until deep golden brown and cooked through, about 3 minutes longer. Using spoons, transfer chicken to large rack set on baking sheet.

Reheat oil to 350°F. Repeat frying with remaining 4 pieces of chicken.

Serve chicken warm or at room temperature within 2 hours, or chill up to 1 day.

SANTA FE TURKEY BURGERS

SERVE THESE ON big buns with the salsa here, or present them on plates with the salsa, refried beans and corn muffins on the side.

4 SERVINGS

12	ounces plum tomatoes, seeded, chopped
½	medium red onion, chopped
⅓	cup finely chopped fresh cilantro
3	large garlic cloves, minced
1	large jalapeño chili, seeded, minced
2	tablespoons olive oil
1	tablespoon red wine vinegar
1	pound ground turkey
1½	teaspoons ground cumin
4	¼-inch-thick slices Monterey Jack cheese (optional)
½	ripe avocado, peeled, diced

Combine first 5 ingredients in medium bowl. Add 1 tablespoon olive oil and vinegar. Season to taste with salt and pepper. Let salsa stand at least 30 minutes, stirring occasionally.

Meanwhile, combine turkey, remaining 1 tablespoon olive oil and cumin. Add 1 cup salsa to turkey mixture and blend well. Form turkey mixture into four 1-inch-thick patties. *(Can be prepared up to 2 hours ahead. Cover and refrigerate burgers and remaining salsa separately.)*

Prepare barbecue (medium-high heat.) Grill burgers until cooked through, about 6 minutes per side, topping with slices of cheese for last 6 minutes, if desired. Mix avocado into remaining salsa. Arrange burgers on platter and serve, passing salsa separately.

SPICED TURKEY BREAST WITH RED CABBAGE SLAW

6 SERVINGS

TURKEY

1½	pounds boneless turkey breast tenderloins
1	large red onion, sliced
3	tablespoons olive oil
1	tablespoon balsamic vinegar
4	bay leaves, halved
1	teaspoon salt
½	teaspoon black pepper
½	teaspoon ground allspice

SLAW

¼	cup olive oil
6	cups finely shredded red cabbage
½	red onion, thinly sliced
3	tablespoons balsamic vinegar
3	tablespoons golden brown sugar
½	teaspoon ground allspice

FOR TURKEY: Place turkey in 1-gallon plastic bag. Add next 7 ingredients. Seal bag and turn several times to blend ingredients. Refrigerate and marinate overnight, turning several times.

FOR SLAW: Heat oil in heavy large skillet over high heat. Add cabbage and onion and cook until cabbage is wilted, stirring, about 3 minutes. Transfer cabbage mixture and all oil from skillet to medium bowl. Mix in vinegar, brown sugar and allspice. Season to taste with salt and pepper. *(Can be prepared 1 day ahead. Cover and refrigerate, tossing occasionally.)*

Prepare barbecue (medium heat). Remove turkey from marinade. Grill until meat thermometer inserted in center registers 165°F, brushing occasionally with marinade, about 8 minutes per side. Transfer turkey to plate. Tent with foil and let stand 10 minutes. Slice turkey diagonally across grain into ¼-inch-thick slices. Mound cabbage in center of platter. Arrange turkey slices around cabbage.

GRILLED RIB-EYE STEAKS WITH YUKON GOLD POTATOES

THE SECRET to this recipe is an olive oil-and-balsamic vinegar marinade that flavors both the steaks and the potatoes.

2 SERVINGS

2	small Yukon Gold potatoes or other baking potatoes (about 6 ounces each)
¼	cup olive oil
1	large shallot, minced
2	large garlic cloves, pressed
1	tablespoon balsamic vinegar
1	tablespoon minced fresh thyme
2	teaspoons minced fresh oregano
1	teaspoon minced fresh rosemary
¼	teaspoon paprika
2	1-inch-thick rib-eye steaks (about 11 ounces each)

Boil potatoes until just tender when pierced with sharp knife, about 12 minutes. Cool. Cut potatoes into ½-inch-thick slices. Transfer to medium bowl; set aside.

Combine olive oil, shallot, garlic, vinegar, thyme, oregano, rosemary and paprika in bowl. Whisk mixture until smooth.

Place steaks in small baking dish. Pour half of olive oil mixture over steaks. Turn steaks to coat evenly. Pour remaining olive oil mixture over potatoes and toss well. Let stand 1 hour at room temperature. *(Steaks and potatoes can be prepared 8 hours ahead. Cover and refrigerate.)*

Prepare barbecue (medium-high heat). Season steaks with salt and pepper. Grill steaks to desired doneness, turning once, about 7 minutes for rare. Transfer to plates. Grill potatoes until brown spots begin to appear, turning once, about 4 minutes. Serve with steaks.

CORIANDER FLANK STEAK

BOTH CORIANDER and cilantro (its fresh herb counterpart) flavor this quick-grilling steak.

4 SERVINGS

2	tablespoons fresh lemon juice
2	tablespoons soy sauce
2	tablespoons olive oil
2	tablespoons ground coriander
2	garlic cloves, minced
1	1½-pound beef flank steak
2	tablespoons chopped fresh cilantro
	Fresh cilantro sprigs

Combine first 5 ingredients in baking dish. Add steak and turn to coat. Cover and refrigerate at least 4 hours or overnight.

Prepare barbecue (high heat). Season steak generously with pepper. Grill until cooked to desired doneness, basting with marinade occasionally, about 4 minutes per side. Transfer to platter. Thinly slice across grain. Sprinkle with chopped cilantro. Garnish with cilantro sprigs.

COMPOSING MENUS

Unless you're a pro at hosting parties, you'll want to keep things simple when it comes time to decide on a menu. Pick a main course first, and make it something that fits the season and the occasion. For summertime meals, fresh-tasting and unfussy food is best, and grilled foods are always welcome. Cooler weather calls for heartier dishes.

Next, decide on side dishes that complement the entrée, and take advantage of all the great produce available from gardens, farmstands and farmers' markets. Try to keep in mind that there should be a balance of textures, shapes and colors on the plate: A delicate grilled fish fillet with cherry tomato salsa would pair nicely with a crunchy green bean salad and perhaps some chewy country bread.

The starters should balance the main course. If there will be a salad or vegetable side dish with cheese, for instance, don't have an hors d'oeuvre that also uses cheese. If you're planning a spicy, strongly flavored entrée, keep the starter more subtle. The dessert should also be planned to work with the rest of the menu. A hearty steak dinner might be best followed by a simple fruit dessert; guests might appreciate a rich and sinful sweet after a lighter main course.

STEAK WITH EGGPLANT, BELL PEPPER AND RADICCHIO

4 SERVINGS

2	cups lightly packed fresh basil leaves
1	cup olive oil
8	large garlic cloves
4	Japanese eggplants
1	1¼-pound top sirloin steak
2	large red bell peppers, quartered
1	large head radicchio, quartered
	Coarsely crumbled feta cheese (optional)
	Fresh lemon wedges
	Basil sprigs

Blend first 3 ingredients in processor until basil is coarsely chopped. Season to taste with salt and pepper. Set basil-oil mixture aside.

Prepare barbecue (medium-high heat). Starting just below stem end, cut each eggplant lengthwise into ¼-inch-thick slices, leaving stem intact. Place eggplants, steak, peppers and radicchio on large baking sheet. Generously rub steak and vegetables (especially eggplant) all over with basil-oil mixture. Season generously with salt and pepper. Grill steak to desired doneness, about 4 minutes per side for medium-rare. Transfer to platter. Tent with foil.

Fan eggplant and arrange on grill. Add bell peppers and grill until vegetables are tender, turning occasionally, about 5 minutes. Transfer to platter. Grill radicchio until slightly wilted, about 30 seconds per side. Transfer to platter.

Cut steak diagonally into slices. Arrange vegetables on side of platter. Sprinkle eggplant with feta, if desired. Garnish with lemon wedges and basil sprigs and serve.

POTATO, BLUE CHEESE AND BEEF SALAD

ROAST BEEF, BLUE CHEESE and red potatoes star in this hearty main-course salad.

4 SERVINGS

2½	pounds red-skinned potatoes
¼	cup dry white wine
⅔	cup mayonnaise
⅔	cup plain yogurt or sour cream
1	tablespoon plus 1 teaspoon Dijon mustard
1	tablespoon plus 1 teaspoon cider vinegar
4	ounces blue cheese, crumbled
¾	cup chopped celery
3	green onions, minced
1	pound sliced roast beef
	Chopped celery leaves

Place potatoes in large pot. Cover with cold water. Boil until tender, about 25 minutes. Drain; cool slightly. Peel potatoes and cut into 1-inch pieces. Transfer to large bowl. Add wine. Season to taste with salt and pepper. Stir gently to coat. Cool. *(Can be prepared 1 day ahead. Cover with plastic and refrigerate.)*

Combine next 7 ingredients in medium bowl. Reserve ⅓ cup mayonnaise mixture. Mix remaining mayonnaise mixture into potatoes. Season to taste with salt and pepper. Mound potato salad in center of plates. Surround with beef. Sprinkle with celery leaves and serve, passing reserved mayonnaise mixture.

MEDITERRANEAN GRILLED LEG OF LAMB

ELEGANT PARTY FARE at its simplest: a butter-flied leg of lamb is marinated overnight, then grilled just ten minutes a side.

8 SERVINGS

1	cup fresh mint leaves
1	cup fresh cilantro
½	cup olive oil
12	large garlic cloves
3	tablespoons ground cumin
2	tablespoons ground coriander
1	tablespoon black pepper
2	teaspoons salt
1	teaspoon cayenne pepper
1	6- to 6½-pound leg of lamb, boned, butterflied, excess fat and connective tissue trimmed

Process first 9 ingredients in processor, stopping occasionally to scrape down sides of processor, until smooth. Spread mixture evenly over both sides of lamb. Transfer lamb to baking sheet; cover with plastic and refrigerate overnight.

Prepare barbecue (medium-high heat). Grill lamb to desired doneness, about 10 minutes per side for medium-rare. Thinly slice lamb across grain. Transfer to platter and serve.

THAI GRILLED LAMB SALAD

TOMATOES AND cucumbers, lime wedges, mint sprigs and sliced grilled lamb make a beautiful salad platter.

4 SERVINGS

2	½-inch-thick leg of lamb steaks or shoulder steaks
¼	cup fresh lime juice
2	tablespoons soy sauce
2	large garlic cloves, pressed
1	teaspoon brown sugar
1	teaspoon chili paste with garlic*
6	tablespoons minced fresh mint
2	green onions, minced
4	tomatoes, sliced
2	cucumbers, peeled, sliced
	Lime wedges
	Fresh mint sprigs

Prepare barbecue (high heat). Season lamb with salt and pepper. Grill until rare, about 3 minutes per side. Transfer to plate. Cool.

Combine lime juice, soy sauce, garlic, brown sugar and chili paste in large bowl. Add any juices from lamb on plate to bowl. Thinly slice lamb. Add lamb to bowl, then mint and onions. Cover and refrigerate until chilled, about 2 hours. *(Can be prepared 6 hours ahead.)*

Place tomato and cucumber slices decoratively around edges of platter. Mound salad in center. Garnish with lime wedges and mint.

*Available at Asian markets and in the Asian foods section of some supermarkets.

GRILLED PORK TENDERLOIN WITH ROASTED GARLIC BUTTER

FIFTEEN GARLIC CLOVES are rendered sweet and creamy after roasting for 20 minutes. They make for a delicious butter, which tops grilled pork tenderloin.

4 SERVINGS

GARLIC BUTTER

15	large garlic cloves (unpeeled)
2	tablespoons olive oil
2	tablespoons (¼ stick) butter, room temperature

PORK

1	large pork tenderloin (about 16 ounces)
1	large garlic clove, minced
1	teaspoon dried marjoram

FOR GARLIC BUTTER: Preheat oven to 350°F. Place garlic in heavy small skillet. Drizzle with olive oil. Bake until garlic is very tender when pierced with sharp knife, about 20 minutes. Cool. Peel garlic and place in small bowl. Add any oil from skillet to bowl. Mash garlic with fork. Mix in butter. Season to taste with salt and pepper. *(Can be prepared 3 days ahead. Cover and refrigerate. Bring to room temperature before continuing.)*

FOR PORK: Prepare barbecue (medium-high heat). Rub tenderloin with garlic and marjoram. Season with salt and pepper. Grill to desired doneness, turning occasionally, about 8 minutes for medium. Transfer pork to platter. Spread with garlic butter and serve.

RIBS WITH MUSTARD-BOURBON SAUCE

THESE AWARD-WINNING ribs spend a night slathered in a spice rub—so you'll want to start the recipe a day ahead.

4 TO 6 SERVINGS

SAUCE

1	tablespoon vegetable oil
2	bunches green onions, chopped
2	cups chopped white onions
8	large garlic cloves, chopped
2	cups (packed) golden brown sugar
1	cup ketchup
1	cup tomato paste (about 9 ounces)
1	cup whole grain Dijon mustard
1	cup water
½	cup Worcestershire sauce
½	cup apple cider vinegar
½	cup apple juice
1	large dried ancho chili,* stemmed, seeded, cut into small pieces
1	tablespoon ground cumin
1½	cups bourbon

SPICE RUB AND RIBS

2	tablespoons ground cumin
1	tablespoon chili powder
1	tablespoon dry mustard
1	tablespoon coarse salt
1½	teaspoons cayenne pepper
1½	teaspoons ground cardamom
1½	teaspoons ground cinnamon
6	pounds baby back pork ribs (about 3 whole racks)

FOR SAUCE: Heat oil in heavy large pot over medium-low heat. Add green onions, white onions and garlic and sauté until tender, about 15 minutes. Mix in all remaining ingredients, adding bourbon last. Simmer sauce until thick and reduced to 7 cups, stirring occasionally, about 1 hour. Season with salt and pepper. *(Sauce can be made 2 weeks ahead. Cover; chill.)*

FOR SPICE RUB AND RIBS: Mix first 7 ingredients in medium bowl. Rub spice mixture over both sides of rib racks. Arrange ribs on large baking sheet. Cover and refrigerate overnight.

Prepare barbecue (medium heat). Cut rib racks into 4- to 6-rib sections. Arrange ribs on barbecue. Grill until meat is tender, occasionally turning ribs with tongs, about 40 minutes. Using tongs, transfer ribs to work surface.

Cut rib sections between bones into individual ribs. Arrange on clean baking sheet. Transfer 3 cups sauce to small bowl; place remaining sauce in small saucepan and reserve. Brush ribs with sauce from bowl.

Return ribs to barbecue. Place pan of reserved sauce at edge of barbecue to rewarm. Grill ribs until brown and crisp on edges, brushing with more sauce from bowl and turning occasionally, about 10 minutes. Transfer ribs to platter. Serve with warm sauce.

*Available at Latin American markets, specialty foods stores and some supermarkets.

HALIBUT WITH FENNEL, SUN-DRIED TOMATOES AND OLIVES

THE DO-AHEAD fennel relish here would also be good with tuna, swordfish, or even chicken.

4 SERVINGS

⅓ cup plus 2 tablespoons olive oil

1 cup finely chopped fennel

1 cup finely chopped leeks (white and light green parts only)

4 large garlic cloves, minced

½ cup dry white wine

1 tablespoon tomato paste

1 pound tomatoes, peeled, seeded, chopped

½ cup chopped drained oil-packed sun-dried tomatoes

⅓ cup pitted sliced Kalamata olives or other brine-cured black olives

4 teaspoons minced fresh rosemary

4 6-ounce halibut fillets (each about 1 inch thick)

Lemon wedges

Fennel fronds

Heat 2 tablespoons oil in heavy large skillet over medium-high heat. Add fennel, leeks and garlic and sauté until crisp-tender, about 5 minutes. Add wine and cook until reduced by half, about 3 minutes. Add tomato paste, chopped tomatoes, sun-dried tomatoes, olives and 1 teaspoon rosemary and cook until slightly thickened. Season to taste with salt and pepper. *(Can be prepared 2 days ahead. Cover and refrigerate. Rewarm over low heat before using.)*

Combine remaining ⅓ cup oil and 3 teaspoons rosemary in small bowl. Arrange halibut

GRILLED PORK CHOPS WITH ITALIAN RELISH

AN EASY TOMATO relish is great over grilled pork chops (pictured above).

4 SERVINGS

¾ pound plum tomatoes, seeded, chopped

¾ cup chopped red onion

¼ cup red wine vinegar

2 tablespoons olive oil

1 tablespoon chopped garlic

1 tablespoon chopped fresh basil or 1 teaspoon dried

1 tablespoon chopped fresh oregano or 1 teaspoon dried

4 ¾- to 1-inch-thick center-cut pork chops

Combine first 7 ingredients in small bowl. Season with salt and pepper. Let stand at least 15 minutes and up to 1 hour.

Prepare barbecue (medium heat). Arrange pork chops in 8 x 8 x 2-inch glass baking dish. Drain liquid from relish; spoon liquid over pork. Let pork marinate at least 15 minutes, turning occasionally. Grill pork until cooked through, about 6 minutes per side.

Transfer pork chops to plates. Spoon relish over and serve immediately.

fillets in single layer in shallow dish. Pour oil-rosemary mixture over. Cover and refrigerate at least 1 hour and up to 4 hours.

Prepare barbecue (medium-high heat). Season halibut with salt and pepper. Grill until fish is just opaque in center, about 7 minutes, turning once. Reheat relish. Arrange fish on plate; spoon relish over. Garnish with lemon wedges and fennel fronds and serve.

GRILLED SWORDFISH TOSTADAS WITH BLACK BEANS

FOR THIS MODERN take on tostadas, black beans, swordfish and an avocado salsa are layered atop grilled tortillas.

4 SERVINGS

BEANS

1	tablespoon olive oil
1	large jalapeño chili, seeded, minced
1	teaspoon chili powder
¾	teaspoon ground cumin
2	15- to 16-ounce cans black beans, rinsed, drained
1	tablespoon fresh lime juice

TOSTADAS

1	cup fresh lime juice
½	cup olive oil
½	cup chopped fresh cilantro
2	12-ounce swordfish steaks
2	medium red onions, cut into ⅓-inch-thick slices
2	red bell peppers, cut into ⅓-inch-thick slices
2	yellow bell peppers, cut into ⅓-inch-thick slices

SALSA

1	cup purchased salsa verde
1	avocado, peeled, pitted, chopped
1	large jalapeño chili, seeded, minced
⅓	cup chopped fresh cilantro
4	7-inch-diameter (fajita-size) flour tortillas
	Lime wedges

FOR BEANS: Heat 1 tablespoon oil in heavy medium saucepan over low heat. Add jalapeño and sauté until tender, about 5 minutes. Add chili powder and cumin and stir 20 seconds. Add beans and lime juice and stir until heated through, mashing beans slightly with spoon, about 3 minutes. *(Can be prepared 1 day ahead. Reheat bean mixture before using.)*

FOR TOSTADAS: Whisk together 1 cup lime juice, ½ cup olive oil and ½ cup cilantro in medium bowl. Arrange swordfish, onions and bell peppers in single layer in large shallow dish. Pour lime juice mixture over. Cover and refrigerate at least 1 hour and up to 3 hours.

FOR SALSA: Combine salsa verde, avocado, jalapeño and cilantro in small bowl. Cover and refrigerate up to 3 hours.

Prepare barbecue (medium-high heat). Season fish and vegetables with salt and pepper. Grill swordfish until just cooked through, about 4 minutes per side. Grill onions and bell peppers until golden and tender, about 4 minutes per side. Cut swordfish into 1-inch pieces. Grill tortillas until crisp, about 2 minutes per side.

Place 1 tortilla on each of 4 plates; spread ¼ of beans over each tortilla; arrange layer of onion slices and bell peppers over. Place swordfish over, dividing equally. Top with avocado-salsa mixture. Garnish tostadas with lime wedges.

SALMON WITH CITRUS-HONEY GLAZE AND GRILLED VEGETABLES

A SIMPLE MARINADE flavors salmon fillets, which are served with a mix of red potatoes, summer squash and asparagus.

2 SERVINGS

6	tablespoons fresh lemon juice
2	tablespoons minced lemon peel
2	tablespoons frozen orange juice concentrate, thawed
4	teaspoons honey
4	tablespoons chopped fresh tarragon
2	6- to 8-ounce (center-cut) salmon fillets
½	pound red-skinned potatoes, halved
6	ounces baby summer squash
6	ounces asparagus, trimmed, cut crosswise in half
1	large leek (white and pale green parts only), cut crosswise into ½-inch-thick slices
⅓	cup olive oil
	Orange slices
	Fresh tarragon sprigs

Whisk together lemon juice, lemon peel, orange juice concentrate, honey and 2 tablespoons tarragon in small bowl. Arrange salmon in single layer in shallow dish. Pour ½ of citrus marinade over; reserve remaining marinade. Cover; chill 1 to 2 hours, turning salmon occasionally.

Place potatoes in steamer basket over boiling water; cover and cook until potatoes are almost tender, about 10 minutes. Transfer potatoes to large shallow dish; add summer squash, asparagus and leek. Combine oil with remaining 2 tablespoons tarragon and pour over vegetables in dish and toss. Season with salt and pepper. Let stand at room temperature 1 hour.

Prepare barbecue (medium-high heat). Season salmon with salt and pepper. Grill vegetables until golden and crisp-tender, about 3 minutes. Grill salmon until cooked through, brushing occasionally with citrus marinade, about 3 minutes per side. Boil remaining marinade in small saucepan until slightly thickened, about 3 minutes. Arrange salmon on plate; brush marinade over. Surround with vegetables. Garnish with orange slices and tarragon sprigs.

TUNA NIÇOISE

IN THIS VERSION of the famous French dish (pictured opposite), the tuna is not canned but fresh and served *under,* not *in,* the salad.

2 SERVINGS

½ cup olive oil

3 tablespoons white wine vinegar

1 tablespoon Dijon mustard

¼ pound small, slender green beans, blanched

1 4- to 5-ounce unpeeled red-skinned potato, cooked, cut into ¼-inch-thick sticks

1 large plum tomato, seeded, cut thinly into vertical strips

⅓ cup Niçois olives*

2 tablespoons drained capers

4 anchovy fillets, chopped

2 7- to 8-ounce tuna steaks (each about ¾ inch thick)

1 hard-boiled egg, cut into wedges

Whisk oil, vinegar and mustard to blend in small bowl. Season with salt and pepper. *(Can be made 1 day ahead. Cover and let stand at room temperature. Rewhisk before using, if necessary.)*

Prepare barbecue (medium-high heat) or preheat broiler. Combine green beans, potato, tomato, olives, capers and anchovies in medium bowl. Toss with enough dressing to coat generously. Season salad to taste with salt and pepper. Brush tuna lightly with dressing. Grill or broil until just cooked through, about 3 minutes per side. Transfer fish to plates. Mound salad on tuna, dividing evenly. Garnish with egg; serve, passing remaining dressing separately.

* Small brine-cured black olives, available at specialty foods stores and in some supermarkets.

INSTANT ENTERTAINING

While it would be lovely to have ample time and energy to prepare everything needed for a dinner party, the reality is that most of us have our hands full just covering the basics. This is where the amazing array of prepared foods and specialty items available today comes into play.

For hors d'oeuvres, use precut or baby vegetables with a purchased cream cheese spread. Even simpler is a bowl of cherry tomatoes to be dipped first into cold vodka, then sea salt. Radishes with butter and salt are another good warm-weather option. Most deli sections have top-quality Italian meats and cheeses and fancy olives; these, along with some artisan breads, make an irresistible antipasto platter.

You can also supplement your menu with take-out dishes like Chinese noodles, Indian samosas and breads, Mexican tamales, and salads and other cold dishes from specialty foods stores. Another sure bet is a cold roast chicken, which will round out any picnic.

For dessert, dress up a purchased angel food cake or pound cake with berries or other fruit and crème fraîche or a mixture of sour cream and whipping cream. Buy cut-up melon, then drizzle it with sparkling wine and sprinkle on a little sugar. Or just offer the freshest fruit and some cheese to finish things up.

GRILLED SCALLOP AND ASPARAGUS SALAD

4 SERVINGS

DRESSING

3	tablespoons balsamic vinegar
1½	tablespoons soy sauce
1	large shallot, minced
1	large garlic clove, minced
1½	teaspoons grated peeled fresh ginger
¾	teaspoon oriental sesame oil
¼	cup plus 2 tablespoons vegetable oil

SALAD

24	jumbo scallops, connective muscle removed
4	tablespoons vegetable oil
1	teaspoon oriental sesame oil
1	pound thin asparagus, ends trimmed
10	cups mixed baby lettuces, torn into bite-size pieces
⅓	cup fresh cilantro leaves

FOR DRESSING: Combine first 6 ingredients in small bowl. Gradually whisk in vegetable oil. *(Dressing can be prepared 3 days ahead; refrigerate.)*

FOR SALAD: Combine scallops, 2 tablespoons vegetable oil and sesame oil in medium bowl. Refrigerate scallops 20 minutes.

Prepare barbecue (medium-high heat). Brush asparagus with remaining 2 tablespoons oil. Grill asparagus and scallops until asparagus is brown and crisp-tender and scallops are just firm, turning occasionally, about 4 minutes. Transfer grilled asparagus and scallops to plate. Drizzle with 3 tablespoons dressing.

Meanwhile, combine lettuces and cilantro in large bowl. Add enough remaining dressing to season to taste. Toss well. Divide salad among plates. Arrange asparagus and scallops decoratively over salad on plates.

BUTTERFLIED SHRIMP WITH CILANTRO-MINT GLAZE

THESE EXOTICALLY flavored shrimp would be good with freshly cooked couscous or rice.

6 SERVINGS

9	tablespoons vegetable oil
6	tablespoons minced fresh cilantro
6	tablespoons minced fresh mint
2	tablespoons minced peeled fresh ginger
6	large garlic cloves, pressed
1	tablespoon white wine vinegar
1	tablespoon sugar
1	tablespoon oriental sesame oil
36	uncooked large shrimp, unpeeled, butterflied

Prepare barbecue (medium-high heat). Mix first 8 ingredients in medium bowl. Season shrimp with salt. Brush mixture over cut side of shrimp. Place shrimp shell side down on grill. Cook until just pink, turning once, about 5 minutes. Brush more glaze over shrimp. Transfer to plates and serve with remaining glaze.

MEDITERRANEAN VEGETARIAN SALAD

A MAIN-COURSE SALAD (pictured at right) brimming with ingredients from the Mediterranean, among them eggplant, zucchini, tomatoes and bell peppers.

4 SERVINGS

½ cup plus 2 tablespoons olive oil

¼ cup red wine vinegar

2 garlic cloves, minced

1 teaspoon dried oregano

2 large Japanese eggplants, diced

2 zucchini, diced

2 14½-ounce cans garbanzo beans (chickpeas), drained

2 large ripe tomatoes, diced

1 cup sliced roasted red peppers from jar

¼ cup minced fresh cilantro

2 green onions, minced

2 tablespoons minced fresh mint

16 romaine lettuce leaves, trimmed

½ pound feta cheese, crumbled

Combine ½ cup olive oil, vinegar, garlic and oregano in medium bowl. Whisk dressing to blend; season with salt and pepper.

Heat remaining 2 tablespoons olive oil in heavy large skillet over medium-low heat. Add eggplants and zucchini and sauté until tender, about 5 minutes. Transfer to large bowl and cool. Season with salt and pepper. *(Can be prepared 1 day ahead. Cover and refrigerate.)*

Add garbanzo beans, tomatoes, peppers, cilantro, green onions and mint to eggplant and zucchini in bowl. Toss with enough dressing to coat. Place 4 lettuce leaves on each of 4 plates to form bed. Divide salad among plates. Sprinkle feta over salads and serve.

SIDE DISHES

New ideas for side-dish favorites (corn, asparagus and potatoes included), along with wonderfully different salads and dressings, make up a selection of great "go-withs."

GRILLED POTATO AND BELL PEPPER PACKETS

DOUBLE OR TRIPLE the ingredients that go into these foil packets, depending on how many people you're serving.

2 SERVINGS

3	medium red-skinned potatoes (unpeeled), thinly sliced
1	medium green bell pepper, cut into thin strips
6	garlic cloves, peeled
4	shallots, peeled and halved lengthwise
3½	tablespoons olive oil
1½	teaspoons minced fresh sage

Prepare barbecue (medium-high heat). Place 2 large sheets of heavy-duty foil on work surface. Combine all ingredients in medium bowl and toss. Divide between foil sheets. Seal packets tightly. Place packets on edge of grill rack; cover grill and cook until potatoes are tender, about 30 minutes. Serve hot.

GRILLED POTATO HALVES

PRECOOKED POTATOES grill in just 15 minutes. A garlic- and herb-flavored oil adds interest.

8 SERVINGS

8	long slender russet potatoes (about 8 ounces each), scrubbed, cut in half lengthwise
4	garlic cloves, chopped
½	teaspoon salt
¼	cup olive oil
1	teaspoon dried oregano

Cook potatoes in pot of boiling salted water until just tender, about 15 minutes. Drain. *(Can be prepared 1 day ahead. Cover and refrigerate. Bring to room temperature before using.)*

Place garlic on work surface. Sprinkle with salt and mash to puree with side of knife. Transfer puree to medium bowl. Add oil and oregano and blend well. Season with pepper. Let stand at least 10 minutes. *(Can be prepared 1 hour ahead. Let stand at room temperature.)* Brush potatoes with seasoned oil. Sprinkle potatoes with salt and pepper to taste.

Prepare barbecue (medium-high heat). Brush potatoes with more seasoned oil and grill until cooked through and slightly charred on all surfaces, occasionally turning and brushing with oil, about 15 minutes. Serve hot.

ORZO PILAF WITH MUSHROOMS, LEEKS AND SUN-DRIED TOMATOES

MAKE THIS MIX of orzo, sun-dried tomatoes, mushrooms, leeks and basil a day ahead, and then bake it just before serving.

8 SERVINGS

	Nonstick vegetable oil spray
1½	cups canned low-salt chicken broth
⅓	cup chopped sun-dried tomatoes (not packed in oil)
1	tablespoon olive oil
12	ounces portobello mushrooms or button mushrooms, stemmed, diced
3	cups sliced leeks (white and pale green parts only)
1	tablespoon chopped garlic
4	cups freshly cooked orzo (rice-shaped pasta; about 1⅓ cups uncooked)
¼	cup chopped fresh basil or 1 tablespoon dried
2	tablespoons balsamic vinegar

Preheat oven to 350°F. Spray 8 x 8 x 2-inch glass baking dish with nonstick spray. Bring broth and tomatoes just to boil in heavy small saucepan. Remove from heat; let stand 10 minutes.

Meanwhile, heat oil in large nonstick skillet over medium heat. Add mushrooms, leeks and garlic. Cover skillet and cook until vegetables are tender, stirring occasionally, about 12 minutes. Remove from heat. Mix in cooked orzo, basil, vinegar, tomatoes and broth. Transfer to prepared baking dish; cover with foil. (*Can be made 1 day ahead; refrigerate.*)

Bake orzo pilaf until heated through, about 40 minutes. Serve pilaf hot.

RISOTTO WITH PEAS AND GREEN ONIONS

CHOPPED GREEN ONIONS and peas add color to the classic rice dish.

4 SERVINGS

3	tablespoons butter
¾	cup chopped green onions
½	teaspoon chopped fresh thyme or ¼ teaspoon dried
¾	cup arborio or medium-grain white rice
2½	cups (or more) canned low-salt chicken broth
¾	cup frozen petite peas, thawed
1	cup grated Parmesan cheese

Melt butter in heavy large saucepan over medium heat. Add green onions and thyme and sauté until onions wilt, about 1 minute. Add rice and stir to coat. Add 2½ cups broth and bring to boil. Reduce heat to medium-low and simmer 15 minutes, stirring occasionally. Mix in peas. Simmer until rice is tender and mixture is creamy, adding more broth by ¼ cupfuls if risotto is dry and stirring often, about 5 minutes. Mix in ⅓ cup cheese; season with salt and pepper. Serve, passing remaining cheese.

SAUTÉED CORN WITH CILANTRO PESTO

COVER THE LEFTOVER pesto with a thin layer of olive oil and keep it in the freezer to use whenever you want to add a big flavor boost to ordinary vegetables.

4 SERVINGS

1   cup (packed) chopped fresh cilantro
2   tablespoons fresh lime juice
¼   cup vegetable oil
¼   cup pine nuts
¼   cup freshly grated Parmesan cheese
3   large garlic cloves
1   teaspoon ground cumin
½   jalapeño chili, chopped
3   cups frozen petite white corn

Puree first 8 ingredients in processor. Season to taste with salt and pepper. *(Pesto can be prepared ahead. Pour thin layer of olive oil over pesto. Cover and refrigerate up to 4 days or freeze up to 2 weeks. Thaw overnight in refrigerator before using.)*

Cook corn according to package instructions; drain. Return corn to saucepan. Add ¼ cup pesto (or more, to taste) and toss over medium-high heat until heated through. Season to taste with salt and pepper.

GRILLED VEGETABLES WITH EIGHT-SPICE SEASONING

YOU CAN PREPARE the spice mixture here up to two weeks ahead and use it with any variety of grill-worthy vegetables.

MAKES ABOUT ¾ CUP SEASONING MIX

3   tablespoons salt
3   tablespoons (packed) golden brown sugar
2   tablespoons paprika
1½   tablespoons chili powder
1   tablespoon black pepper
2¼   teaspoons garlic powder
1½   teaspoons cayenne pepper
1½   teaspoons dried basil
     Assorted vegetables (such as zucchini, bell peppers, red onions and large mushrooms)
     Olive oil

Combine first 8 ingredients in processor. Blend 15 seconds. Transfer to small jar; cover tightly. *(Can be prepared 2 weeks ahead. Store in refrigerator.)*

Prepare barbecue (medium-high heat) or preheat broiler. Cut all vegetables into ½-inch-thick slices. Brush with olive oil. Sprinkle generously with spice mixture. Grill until just cooked through, turning occasionally, about 8 minutes.

ASPARAGUS WITH PARMESAN BUTTER

A PARMESAN-FLAVORED butter tops crisp-tender asparagus spears, which are briefly broiled before serving.

4 SERVINGS

1	pound asparagus, ends trimmed
3	tablespoons butter, room temperature
½	cup (packed) grated Parmesan cheese (about 2 ½ ounces)
1	tablespoon chopped fresh basil or 1 teaspoon dried
1	large garlic clove, chopped
1½	teaspoons fresh lemon juice

Cook asparagus in large pot of boiling salted water until just crisp-tender, about 3 minutes. Drain thoroughly. Arrange asparagus on broiler-proof platter. Set aside.

Preheat broiler. Beat butter in medium bowl until fluffy. Beat in cheese, basil, garlic and lemon juice. Season with salt and pepper. Drop butter mixture by teaspoonfuls over asparagus.

Broil asparagus until topping browns, watching closely to avoid burning, about 3 minutes. Serve asparagus hot.

BEYOND THE BASKET

A classic wicker picnic basket is charming and practical, but there are numerous other ways to get your meal from the kitchen to the particular outdoor location of choice.

A large canvas boating tote is sturdy enough for a heavy load. Besides transporting a good amount of food, a tin washtub or a red wagon will add some whimsy to the excursion. Wooden crates with handles can hold a lot, too; old-fashioned ones used to carry milk, wine or fruits and vegetables, can be picked up at flea markets and antique shops.

A wheelbarrow can come in handy; use it to bring along just about everything, or fill it with ice and drinks. Plastic tubs in a variety of colors are available at home-supply and hardware stores; they're especially useful for ice, and their light weight is an added bonus.

If it's a picnic involving a substantial hike, your best bet is to travel light and use a backpack. Put the heaviest items at the bottom to make the load more secure, and wrap anything breakable or with sharp edges in dish towels or cloth napkins.

GREEN SALAD WITH APPLE DRESSING AND CAMEMBERT TOASTS

THIS MAKES A good after-dinner salad (pictured above), served between the main course and dessert in the French style.

4 SERVINGS

3 tablespoons apple cider vinegar

3 tablespoons walnut oil

1 large Red Delicious apple, cored, cut into ½-inch pieces

4 ounces Camembert cheese, rind trimmed

8 thin diagonal baguette slices, lightly toasted

8 cups mixed salad greens (such as curly endive, romaine and radicchio; about 5 ounces)

Whisk vinegar and oil in large bowl to blend. Season with salt and pepper. Stir in apple. Let apple marinate at room temperature 30 minutes, stirring occasionally.

Spread Camembert cheese evenly over baguette toasts, dividing equally.

Add greens to apple dressing; toss to coat. Season with salt and pepper. Divide among plates and serve with cheese toasts.

ITALIAN SALAD WITH BLUE CHEESE

RADICCHIO AND ARUGULA combine with fennel and basil in this easy salad. Toasted pine nuts add crunch.

4 SERVINGS

½ cup olive oil

3 tablespoons balsamic vinegar

1 tablespoon Dijon mustard

1 head radicchio, torn into bite-size pieces

1 fennel bulb, halved lengthwise, thinly sliced

½ small red onion, thinly sliced

4 bunches fresh arugula, trimmed

½ cup chopped fresh basil

½ cup pine nuts, toasted

4 ounces blue cheese, crumbled

Whisk first 3 ingredients in small bowl to blend. Set aside. Mix all remaining ingredients in large bowl. *(Can be made 1 day ahead. Cover dressing and salad separately and refrigerate. Rewhisk dressing before continuing.)* Add dressing to salad; toss well to coat. Season with salt and pepper and serve.

CURRIED COUSCOUS SALAD

THIS WOULD BE nice with grilled chicken breasts. Make it up to two days ahead and serve it straight from the refrigerator.

4 TO 6 SERVINGS

1½ cups water

1 teaspoon curry powder

½ teaspoon salt

1 cup couscous

¼ cup olive oil

3 tablespoons fresh lemon juice

⅓ cup dried currants

¼ cup chopped fresh cilantro

¼ cup chopped green onions

Bring first 3 ingredients to boil in heavy medium saucepan. Mix in couscous. Remove from heat. Cover and let stand 5 minutes. Fluff couscous with fork. Mix oil and lemon juice in large bowl. Add couscous and remaining ingredients and toss gently. Season to taste with pepper. Cover and refrigerate until cold, at least 2 hours. *(Can be prepared 2 days ahead. Keep chilled.)*

GRAPEFRUIT, AVOCADO AND FENNEL SALAD

A COMPOSED SALAD, this delicious dish (pictured below) mixes both tart and sweet flavors.

8 SERVINGS

⅓ cup fresh orange juice

¼ cup fresh lemon juice

3 tablespoons olive oil

2 tablespoons honey

1 tablespoon minced shallot

1 teaspoon grated lemon peel

1 teaspoon grated orange peel

1 teaspoon minced peeled fresh ginger

1 teaspoon dry mustard

1 teaspoon oriental sesame oil

2 large pink grapefruits, peel and white pith removed

1 pound fennel bulbs, trimmed, cut into paper-thin slices

2 large avocados, halved, pitted, peeled, cut into thin slices

2 cups arugula

Whisk first 10 ingredients in large bowl to blend. Season with salt and pepper.

Using sharp knife, cut between membranes of grapefruits to release segments.

Spread fennel slices over large platter. Arrange grapefruit segments and avocado slices atop fennel. Drizzle dressing over salad. Arrange arugula atop salad and serve.

DESSERTS

Pies and tarts, cakes and custards, fruit and frozen desserts, cookies and brownies—there's something here for every sweet tooth and every outdoor occasion, party to picnic.

DEEP-DISH APPLE PIE WITH CHEDDAR CRUST

INSTEAD OF A bottom crust, this old-fashioned pie has a cheesy top crust. That, and the fact that it's baked in an oval dish, make it resemble a fruit cobbler.

8 SERVINGS

CRUST

2½ cups unbleached all purpose flour

½ teaspoon salt

½ cup chilled solid vegetable shortening, cut into pieces

6 tablespoons (¾ stick) chilled unsalted butter, cut into ½-inch pieces

6 ounces extra-sharp cheddar cheese, coarsely shredded

⅔ cup (about) ice water

FRUIT

4 pounds Granny Smith apples, peeled, cored, thinly sliced

⅔ cup raisins

½ cup (packed) golden brown sugar

⅓ cup plus 2 teaspoons sugar

3 tablespoons unbleached all purpose flour

2 tablespoons fresh lemon juice

¾ teaspoon ground cinnamon

½ teaspoon ground ginger

¼ teaspoon ground nutmeg

3 tablespoons unsalted butter, cut into small pieces

1 egg, beaten to blend with 1 tablespoon water (for glaze)

FOR CRUST: Blend flour and salt in processor. Add shortening and butter and cut in using several on/off turns. Add cheese and cut in until shortening and butter resemble small peas. With machine running, gradually blend in enough water to form soft moist clumps. Gather dough into ball; flatten into disk. Wrap in plastic and chill at least 2 hours and up to 2 days. *(Can be frozen up to 2 weeks. Let stand at room temperature to soften before continuing.)*

FOR FRUIT: Mix apples, raisins, brown sugar, ⅓ cup sugar, flour, lemon juice and spices in large bowl. Let stand 30 minutes.

Preheat oven to 400°F. Remove dough from refrigerator; let stand 15 minutes. Spoon fruit and any accumulated juices into 13 x 9-inch oval baking dish. Dot fruit with butter.

Roll out dough on floured surface to oval about ½ inch larger than baking dish. Fold in ½ inch of edge to form double-thick border; crimp. Cut out 1-inch-wide hole from center of crust. Using tart pan bottom as aid, lift dough and place atop fruit. Tuck in around edges.

Bake pie 15 minutes. Brush crust with egg glaze. Top with remaining 2 teaspoons sugar. Reduce oven temperature to 375°F. Bake pastry until golden, about 35 minutes. Cool on rack 15 minutes. Serve pie warm.

CHOCOLATE BROWNIE TART

THIS DESSERT (pictured at right) is made with a cookie crust and a brownie filling. (White chocolate drizzled over the top gives it an elegant "restaurant" look.)

12 SERVINGS

CRUST

- 1 cup all purpose flour
- 2 tablespoons (packed) golden brown sugar
- 1 ounce unsweetened chocolate, chopped
  Pinch of salt
- 6 tablespoons (¾ stick) chilled unsalted butter, cut into pieces
- 2 tablespoons milk
- 1 teaspoon vanilla extract

FILLING

- ½ cup (1 stick) unsalted butter, room temperature
- 3 ounces unsweetened chocolate, chopped
- 3 ounces semisweet chocolate, chopped
- 1½ cups sugar
- 3 large eggs
- 2 teaspoons vanilla extract
- ⅛ teaspoon salt
- ¾ cup all purpose flour
- ½ cup chopped pecans, toasted

TOPPING

- 2 ounces semisweet chocolate, chopped
- ¼ cup (½ stick) unsalted butter
- 1 teaspoon vegetable oil
- 2 ounces good-quality white chocolate (such as Lindt or Baker's), chopped

FOR CRUST: Blend first 4 ingredients in processor until finely chopped. Add butter; cut in using on/off turns until mixture resembles coarse meal. Add milk and vanilla; process until moist clumps form. Using plastic wrap as aid, press dough over bottom and up sides of 11-inch-diameter tart pan with removable bottom. Freeze tart crust for 30 minutes.

Preheat oven to 350°F. Bake crust until just set and beginning to brown around edges, about 8 minutes. Transfer pan to rack and cool crust completely. Maintain oven temperature.

FOR FILLING: Stir butter and chocolates in medium saucepan over low heat until melted. Cool slightly. Beat sugar, eggs, vanilla and salt in medium bowl until fluffy, about 4 minutes. Whisk in chocolate. Mix in flour and nuts.

Pour batter into crust. Bake until filling puffs around edges and tester inserted into center comes out with moist crumbs attached, 40 minutes. Transfer to rack; cool completely.

FOR TOPPING: Stir semisweet chocolate, butter and oil in small saucepan over low heat until melted. Spread mixture over tart. Refrigerate until set, about 15 minutes.

Stir white chocolate in top of double boiler over simmering water until melted. Drizzle atop tart. Refrigerate until set, about 10 minutes. *(Can be made 1 day ahead. Cover and refrigerate.)* Serve tart at room temperature.

LEMON MERINGUE PIE WITH HAZELNUT SHORTBREAD CRUST

HERE's A FOOLPROOF version (pictured at right) of the classic pie. Using powdered sugar for the meringue instead of granulated sugar is the secret to a perfect topping.

MAKES ONE 9-INCH PIE

CRUST

⅓ cup hazelnuts, toasted, husked

1¼ cups all purpose flour

½ cup (1 stick) unsalted butter, cut into pieces, room temperature

½ cup powdered sugar

1 large egg yolk

1 tablespoon grated lemon peel

½ teaspoon salt

FILLING

1½ cups water

1 cup sugar

½ cup fresh lemon juice

6 large egg yolks

5 tablespoons cornstarch

2 tablespoons grated lemon peel

¼ teaspoon salt

2 tablespoons (¼ stick) unsalted butter

MERINGUE

7 large egg whites

½ teaspoon cream of tartar

1⅔ cups powdered sugar

FOR CRUST: Grind nuts finely in processor. Add flour and blend well. Add remaining ingredients. Using on/off turns, process just until moist clumps form. Turn dough out onto lightly floured surface. Gather dough into ball; flatten into disk. Wrap in plastic; chill until firm enough to roll, about 45 minutes.

Position rack in center of oven; preheat to 325°F. Roll out dough between sheets of waxed paper to 12-inch round, turning over occasionally to lift and smooth paper. Peel off top sheet. Using bottom paper as aid, lift dough and invert into 9-inch-diameter glass pie dish. Peel off paper. Press dough gently into dish. Fold overhang under; crimp to form decorative edge. Pierce crust all over with fork. Chill 15 minutes.

Line crust with foil. Fill with dried beans or pie weights. Bake crust until sides are set, about 15 minutes. Remove foil and beans. Bake until crust is pale golden, about 20 minutes longer. Transfer crust to rack and cool completely. Reduce oven temperature to 300°F.

FOR FILLING: Whisk first 7 ingredients in heavy medium saucepan to blend. Using whisk, stir over medium heat until filling thickens and just begins to boil, about 20 minutes. Remove saucepan from heat. Whisk in butter. Spoon hot filling into prepared crust.

FOR MERINGUE: Using electric mixer, beat egg whites in large stainless steel bowl at low speed until foamy. Beat in cream of tartar and 1 tablespoon powdered sugar. Gradually beat in remaining sugar, 1 tablespoon at a time. Beat at medium speed until stiff glossy peaks form, about 8 minutes. Spread meringue over warm filling, covering completely, sealing meringue to crust edges and mounding in center.

Bake pie for 30 minutes. Reduce oven temperature to 275°F and continue to bake until meringue is golden brown and set when pie is shaken slightly, about 50 minutes. Transfer pie to rack and cool completely, about 4 hours. *(Can be made 1 day ahead. Refrigerate uncovered.)*

PEAR AND GINGER UPSIDE-DOWN CAKE

SERVE THIS HOMESTYLE favorite with sweetened whipped cream, if you like.

8 SERVINGS

	Nonstick vegetable oil spray
1½	cups cake flour
1	tablespoon plus ¾ teaspoon ground cinnamon
2	teaspoons ground ginger
1⅛	teaspoons baking powder
½	teaspoon salt
½	teaspoon black pepper
¼	teaspoon ground cloves
¼	teaspoon ground allspice
¼	teaspoon baking soda
½	cup whole milk
¾	teaspoon vanilla extract
½	cup (1 stick) unsalted butter, room temperature
½	cup (packed) golden brown sugar
1	large egg
½	cup mild-flavored (light) molasses
3	firm but ripe Bosc pears, peeled, cored, thinly sliced

Preheat oven to 350°F. Spray 9-inch-diameter cake pan with 2-inch-high sides with nonstick spray. Sift flour and next 8 ingredients into medium bowl. Combine milk and vanilla in glass measuring cup. Beat butter and sugar in large bowl until light and fluffy. Add egg and beat until well blended. Add molasses and beat well. Mix in dry ingredients alternately with milk mixture, beginning and ending with dry ingredients. Arrange sliced pears in bottom of prepared pan. Pour batter over.

Bake cake until tester inserted into center comes out clean, about 40 minutes. Transfer pan to rack and cool 10 minutes. Using small knife, cut around sides of pan to loosen cake. Turn cake out onto rack and cool slightly. *(Can be made 1 day ahead. Cover; keep at room temperature.)*

Serve warm or at room temperature.

BANANA LAYER CAKE WITH CREAM CHEESE FROSTING

WITH MASHED BANANAS in the cake batter and sliced bananas between the layers, this dessert is a banana lover's dream.

8 TO 10 SERVINGS

2¼	cups cake flour
¾	teaspoon baking soda
½	teaspoon baking powder
½	teaspoon plus pinch of salt
1	cup mashed ripe bananas (about 2 large)
¼	cup buttermilk
1	teaspoon plus 1 tablespoon vanilla extract
1½	cups (3 sticks) unsalted butter, room temperature
1⅓	cups sugar
2	large eggs
2	8-ounce packages cream cheese, room temperature
1½	cups powdered sugar
2	large bananas, peeled, sliced

Preheat oven to 350°F. Lightly butter three 8-inch-diameter cake pans with 2-inch-high sides; dust pans with flour. Combine cake flour, baking soda, baking powder and ½ teaspoon salt in medium bowl. Mix mashed bananas, buttermilk and 1 teaspoon vanilla in another medium bowl. Using electric mixer, beat ½ cup butter and sugar in large bowl until blended. Add eggs 1 at a time, beating to blend after each addition. Add dry ingredients alternately with banana mixture in 3 additions, beginning and ending with dry ingredients and beating just until blended after each addition. Divide batter equally among prepared pans.

Bake cakes until tops are just beginning to color and tester inserted into center comes out with a few crumbs attached, about 20 minutes. Cool cakes in pans on racks 10 minutes. Using small knife, cut around cakes to loosen; turn cakes out onto racks and cool completely. *(Can be made ahead. Wrap cake layers separately with plastic; freeze up to 2 weeks. Thaw 4 hours at room temperature before continuing.)*

Beat cream cheese and remaining 1 cup butter in large bowl until light and fluffy. Beat in remaining 1 tablespoon vanilla and pinch of salt. Gradually beat in powdered sugar. Cover and refrigerate frosting until firm enough to spread, about 15 minutes.

Place 1 cake layer on platter. Spread ½ cup frosting over top. Place half of sliced bananas evenly over frosting, leaving ¼-inch border at edge. Place second cake layer on work surface. Spread ¼ cup frosting over top. Place cake layer, frosting side down, atop bananas. Spread ½ cup frosting over top. Place remaining half of sliced bananas evenly over frosting, leaving ¼-inch border at edge. Place third cake layer on work surface. Spread ¼ cup frosting over top. Place cake layer, frosting side down, atop bananas. Spread remaining frosting over sides and top of cake. *(Can be made 1 day ahead. Cover and chill. Let stand 1 hour at room temperature before serving.)*

GRILLED POUND CAKE WITH CHOCOLATE-HONEY SAUCE

ELEGANT *AND* EASY, this dessert combines purchased pound cake and a homemade honey-sweetened chocolate sauce.

8 SERVINGS

8	ounces bittersweet (not unsweetened) or semisweet chocolate, chopped
½	cup (1 stick) unsalted butter
3	tablespoons honey
1	12-ounce pound cake, cut into 12 slices
⅓	cup orange liqueur
	Vanilla ice cream
½	cup coarsely chopped toasted pecans
2½	teaspoons grated orange peel

Stir chocolate, butter and honey in top of double boiler set over simmering water until melted and smooth. *(Sauce can be prepared 3 days ahead. Cool completely. Cover and refrigerate. Stir in top of double boiler until heated through before using.)*

Prepare barbecue (medium heat). Working in batches, toast pound cake slices on barbecue grill or in electric toaster until golden. Generously brush both sides of cake slices with liqueur. Cut pound cake slices diagonally in half, forming triangles.

Drizzle warm chocolate-honey sauce on plates. Scoop ice cream atop sauce. Place 3 cake triangles on each plate. Sprinkle with pecans and orange peel and serve.

GRAND MARNIER CUSTARD WITH STRAWBERRIES

A LOVELY YET simple dessert that can be made ahead. Serve it in glass bowls or parfait glasses.

2 SERVINGS

¼	cup whipping cream
3	tablespoons sugar
1	large egg
1	large egg yolk
2	tablespoons Grand Marnier or other orange liqueur
2	tablespoons fresh orange juice
1	tablespoon fresh lemon juice
1	teaspoon grated orange peel
1	1-pint basket strawberries, hulled, sliced
2	sprigs fresh mint

Whisk first 8 ingredients to blend in heavy medium saucepan. Whisk over medium heat until mixture thickens and comes to a gentle simmer. Transfer to bowl; cover and chill. *(Can be prepared up to 2 days ahead.)*

Divide berries between 2 glass bowls or parfait glasses. Spoon custard over berries, dividing equally. Garnish with mint and serve.

LEMON CRÈME CARAMEL

BEGIN PREPARING these custards (pictured at right) at least one day ahead. Garnish them with twists of lemon peel for that extra touch.

6 SERVINGS

¾ cup sugar

3 tablespoons water

1 cup milk

¾ cup whipping cream

2 large eggs

1 large egg yolk

2 teaspoons vanilla extract

1 teaspoon finely grated lemon peel

Preheat oven to 325°F. Combine ½ cup sugar and 3 tablespoons water in heavy small skillet. Stir over medium heat until sugar dissolves. Increase heat to medium-high and boil until syrup is deep amber, brushing down sides of pan with wet pastry brush and swirling pan occasionally, about 6 minutes. Immediately pour hot caramel into six ½-cup soufflé dishes or custard cups, dividing equally. Swirl soufflé dishes to evenly coat bottoms with caramel.

Bring milk and cream to boil. Remove from heat. Whisk eggs, yolk and ¼ cup sugar in medium bowl to blend. Pour in hot milk mixture. Stir in vanilla and lemon peel. Place dishes in large roasting pan. Divide mixture among prepared dishes. Add enough hot water to come 1 inch up sides of dishes. Bake until custards are just set, about 35 minutes. Remove from water; cool. Refrigerate overnight. *(Can be prepared 2 days ahead. Cover with plastic and keep refrigerated.)*

Run small sharp knife around edges of custards. Invert onto plates and serve.

MINT CHOCOLATE ICE CREAM CAKE

8 SERVINGS

1 16-ounce package chocolate sandwich cookies

3 tablespoons unsalted butter, melted

1 quart mint chocolate chip ice cream

1 quart cookies-and-cream ice cream

1 10-ounce package mint chocolate chips

Finely grind cookies in processor. Blend in melted butter. Press crumb mixture evenly onto bottom and 2¼ inches up sides of 9-inch-diameter springform pan with 2¾-inch-high sides. Refrigerate 30 minutes.

Meanwhile, soften mint ice cream slightly, about 2 minutes in microwave set on medium-low or in refrigerator. Spread mint ice cream evenly in chilled crust. Freeze until set but not solid, about 1 hour.

Soften cookies-and-cream ice cream. Spread evenly over mint ice cream in pan. Freeze at least 2 hours or up to 3 days. Melt chocolate chips in top of double boiler over simmering water, stirring until smooth. Using fork, lightly drizzle some chocolate back and forth over cake, creating design. Release sides of pan. Cut cake into wedges. Serve, passing remaining melted chocolate chips separately as sauce.

FROZEN
PEANUT BUTTER PIE

PREPARE THIS kid-pleasing pie up to four days ahead—and then mark it off your list of things to do before the party.

8 SERVINGS

¾ cup graham cracker crumbs

1 cup sugar

2 tablespoons (packed) golden brown sugar

¼ cup (½ stick) unsalted butter, melted

1 8-ounce package cream cheese, room temperature

1 cup creamy peanut butter (do not use old-fashioned style or freshly ground)

1 tablespoon vanilla extract

1½ cups chilled whipping cream

Purchased hot fudge sauce

Mix graham cracker crumbs, ¼ cup sugar and brown sugar in medium bowl. Add butter and stir until blended. Press mixture onto bottom and up sides of 9-inch-diameter glass pie dish. Refrigerate while preparing filling.

Beat cream cheese, peanut butter, vanilla and remaining ¾ cup sugar in large bowl until smooth. Using electric mixer with clean dry beaters, beat cream in another large bowl until stiff peaks form. Gently fold whipped cream into peanut butter mixture in 4 additions. Spoon filling into prepared crust, mounding in center. Freeze until firm, about 2 hours. *(Can be prepared 4 days ahead. Cover and keep frozen.)*

Warm hot fudge sauce according to package directions, if desired. Cut pie into wedges; serve with hot fudge sauce.

FRESH FRUIT WITH
GRANOLA TOPPING

THIS QUICK, UNBAKED fruit "crisp" is made by sprinkling a crunchy, low-fat granola over sliced fresh summer fruits.

4 SERVINGS

GRANOLA

2 cups old-fashioned or quick-cooking oats

¾ cup sliced almonds

½ cup raisins

¼ cup honey

1 tablespoon vegetable oil

½ teaspoon ground cinnamon

FRUIT

2 nectarines, pitted, sliced

2 plums, pitted, sliced

½ 1-pint basket strawberries, hulled

½ ½-pint basket blueberries

3 tablespoons orange juice

FOR GRANOLA: Preheat oven to 350°F. Combine oats, sliced almonds and raisins in 13 x 9-inch baking pan. Bring honey, oil and cinnamon to boil in heavy small saucepan, stirring constantly. Pour over oat mixture and stir until evenly distributed. Bake granola until golden, stirring frequently, about 18 minutes. Cool in pan. Crumble granola into pieces. Store airtight at room temperature. *(Can be made 2 weeks ahead.)*

FOR FRUIT: Toss nectarines, plums, berries and orange juice in medium bowl. Let stand 20 minutes at room temperature.

Divide fruit among dishes. Sprinkle each serving with about ¼ cup granola (reserve remaining granola for another use).

RED PLUM CRUNCH

THE SEASON'S BEST plums get topped with a mix of oats, brown sugar and cinnamon.

8 SERVINGS

TOPPING

1	cup all purpose flour
¾	cup old-fashioned oats
¾	cup (packed) golden brown sugar
2½	teaspoons ground cinnamon
¾	cup (1½ sticks) chilled unsalted butter, cut into pieces
1	large egg, beaten to blend

FRUIT

3	pounds red plums (such as Santa Rosa), halved, pitted, cut into ¾-inch-wide wedges
¾	cup (packed) golden brown sugar
¼	cup crème de cassis (black currant-flavored liqueur; optional)
2	tablespoons all purpose flour
	Whipped cream

FOR TOPPING: Mix flour, oats, brown sugar and ground cinnamon in large bowl. Add chilled butter and rub in with fingertips until mixture resembles coarse meal. Add egg and toss until mixture forms small moist clumps (do not overmix). *(Topping can be prepared 8 hours ahead. Cover tightly and refrigerate.)*

FOR FRUIT: Preheat oven to 375°F. Toss plums, sugar, cassis and flour in large bowl to blend. Transfer to 13 x 9 x 2-inch glass baking dish. Sprinkle topping over. Bake until fruit bubbles and thickens and topping is crisp and brown, about 45 minutes. Cool. *(Can be prepared 8 hours ahead. Cover loosely; keep at room temperature.)* Serve with whipped cream.

OATMEAL-RAISIN DROP COOKIES

DATES, RAISINS AND chopped nuts make these big, wholesome cookies truly irresistible.

MAKES ABOUT 5 DOZEN

2	cups all purpose flour
1½	teaspoons ground cinnamon
1	teaspoon salt
1	teaspoon baking soda
¼	teaspoon ground cloves
1¼	cups (packed) dark brown sugar
1	cup (2 sticks) unsalted butter, room temperature
⅓	cup dark corn syrup
1	large egg
2	teaspoons vanilla extract
2	cups old-fashioned oats
1	cup chopped pitted dates
1	cup raisins
¾	cup chopped pecans or walnuts

Preheat oven to 350°F. Butter 2 large baking sheets. Sift flour, cinnamon, salt, baking soda and cloves into medium bowl. Using electric mixer, beat sugar and butter in large bowl until well blended. Beat in corn syrup, egg and vanilla. Mix in flour mixture. Add oats, dates, raisins and nuts; stir to blend.

Drop dough by generous tablespoonfuls onto prepared sheets, spacing 2 inches apart. Bake until cookies are golden brown on edges, about 15 minutes. Transfer cookies to racks and cool. *(Can be made ahead. Store in airtight container at room temperature 3 days or freeze up to 2 weeks.)*

MOCHA CHEESECAKE BROWNIE BARS

THE BROWNIE CRUST and cream cheese filling need to refrigerate overnight before the sour cream topping gets added.

MAKES 24

BROWNIE

¼ cup (½ stick) unsalted butter

2 ounces semisweet chocolate, coarsely chopped

⅓ cup unbleached all purpose flour

⅓ cup sugar

1 large egg

½ teaspoon vanilla extract

Pinch of salt

FILLING

⅓ cup whipping cream

1½ tablespoons instant coffee powder

8 ounces cream cheese, room temperature

⅔ cup sugar

1 large egg

1 large egg yolk

¼ cup sour cream

1 tablespoon all purpose flour

½ teaspoon vanilla extract

⅓ cup miniature semisweet chocolate chips

TOPPING

1 cup sour cream

⅓ cup powdered sugar

FOR BROWNIE: Preheat oven to 350°F. Butter and flour 8 x 8 x 2-inch baking pan. Melt butter in medium saucepan over low heat. Add chocolate; stir until chocolate melts. Remove from heat. Whisk in remaining ingredients. Spread batter in thin layer on bottom of pan. Bake until tester inserted into center comes out with moist crumbs attached, about 10 minutes. Cool.

FOR FILLING: Reduce oven temperature to 325°F. Stir cream and coffee powder in small saucepan over medium-high heat until coffee powder dissolves. Cool.

Beat cream cheese and sugar in large bowl until light. Beat in egg and yolk. Add sour cream, flour, vanilla and coffee mixture; beat until smooth. Stir in chocolate chips. Spoon filling evenly over brownie. Bake until filling puffs slightly around edges and center is set, about 35 minutes. Cool completely on rack. Cover pan with foil and chill overnight.

FOR TOPPING: Stir sour cream and sugar in small saucepan over low heat until sugar dissolves, about 2 minutes (do not boil). Spread topping evenly over filling. Cool slightly. Cover; chill until topping sets, at least 2 hours. *(Can be made 1 day ahead; keep chilled.)* Cut into 24 bars.

PICNICS

HOT SPICED CIDER

LENTIL SOUP WITH
ANDOUILLE SAUSAGE

CHEDDAR CHEESE POTATO BREAD

MAPLE-CINNAMON CAKE

Menu for Six

othing tastes better than food eaten outdoors after some kind of appetite-inducing activity. When you join friends to go cross-country skiing, everyone is guaranteed clean air, beautiful scenery and plenty of exercise. With this menu along for the ride, good food is a given too.

Steaming cider, spiced with cinnamon, cloves and nutmeg, will help warm everyone up from the inside out, as will bowls of hearty lentil soup with chunks of sausage. Homemade potato bread is the perfect go-with, and squares of maple-flavored cake round out the hearty lunch menu. Everything can be made ahead, leaving only some rewarming and the packing up to do before you hit the trails.

All you need to pull off this winter picnic are a couple of thermoses to hold the cider and the soup, some unbreakable heatproof bowls and cups (tin or flexible plastic camping ware works well), utensils, napkins and something waterproof to sit on (plastic tarps, neoprene pads or even one of those new lightweight, inflatable mattress pads), along with a couple of backpacks designed with skiers in mind. Available for rent at many ski and sports shops, they are light and fit close to the body so that they move with you. With a good pack and equitable distribution of the food, you'll hardly know you're carrying it.

And if it should cloud up while you're out on the trail, just remember: You're prepared, so sip, snack and let it snow.

HOT SPICED CIDER

6 SERVINGS

2	quarts apple juice
¼	cup plus 2 tablespoons frozen orange juice concentrate
¼	cup plus 2 tablespoons frozen lemonade concentrate
¼	teaspoon (generous) ground cinnamon
¼	teaspoon (generous) ground cloves
¼	teaspoon (generous) ground nutmeg

Combine all ingredients in heavy large pot and bring to boil. Reduce heat and simmer 45 minutes. *(Can be prepared 1 week ahead. Cool, cover and refrigerate. Bring cider to simmer. Cool slightly, then pour into thermos to transport.)*

LENTIL SOUP WITH ANDOUILLE SAUSAGE

6 SERVINGS

4½	cups chicken stock or canned low-salt chicken broth
4½	cups beef stock or canned beef broth
1½	cups dried lentils
2	teaspoons fennel seeds
2	tablespoons olive oil
⅓	cup chopped celery
⅓	cup chopped carrot
⅓	cup chopped onion
6	ounces andouille sausage,* halved lengthwise, cut into ½-inch pieces
2	teaspoons dried thyme
½	teaspoon Creole seasoning

Combine both stocks and lentils in large pot over high heat. Bring to boil. Reduce heat, cover and simmer lentil mixture 30 minutes.

Meanwhile, heat medium skillet over medium heat. Add fennel seeds; sauté until seeds are light golden brown, about 2 minutes. Remove fennel seeds from skillet.

Heat oil in same skillet over medium heat. Add chopped celery, carrot and onion; sauté until onion is translucent and celery and carrot are tender, about 5 minutes.

Add toasted fennel seeds, sautéed vegetables, sausage, thyme and Creole seasoning to soup. Cover and simmer until lentils are very tender, stirring occasionally, about 45 minutes. Season soup to taste with salt and pepper. *(Can be prepared ahead. Cover and chill 2 days or freeze up to 2 weeks. Thaw overnight in refrigerator if frozen. Rewarm over medium heat, stirring occasionally. Transport soup in thermos.)*

A smoked pork-and-beef sausage, available at specialty foods stores. Smoked bratwurst, kielbasa or smoked Hungarian sausage can be substituted.

CHEDDAR CHEESE POTATO BREAD

MAKES 1 LOAF

1	cup evaporated milk, room temperature
½	cup warm water (125°F to 130°F)
3	tablespoons vegetable oil
2	envelopes fast-rising dry yeast
2	tablespoons sugar
1	tablespoon salt
½	teaspoon hot pepper sauce
2	cups grated red-skinned potatoes (about 2 medium)
2	cups firmly packed grated sharp cheddar cheese (about 8 ounces)
5	cups (about) unbleached all purpose flour
	Cornmeal

Lightly brush large bowl with oil. Add milk, ½ cup warm water, 3 tablespoons oil, yeast, sugar, salt and hot pepper sauce to bowl. Stir until yeast dissolves. Mix in potatoes and 1½ cups cheese. Gradually mix in enough flour to form soft dough. Knead dough on lightly floured surface until smooth and elastic, adding more flour if sticky, about 8 minutes. Cover with towel; let dough rest for 15 minutes.

Oil 12-inch-diameter pizza pan. Sprinkle pan generously with cornmeal. Knead dough 1 minute. Form into 6-inch-diameter round. Transfer to prepared pan. Brush loaf with oil. Cover with plastic, then with towel. Place in warm draft-free area. Let stand until almost doubled in volume, about 1 hour.

Preheat oven to 400°F. Using large sharp knife, score large *X* through top of loaf. Bake 40 minutes. Reduce oven temperature to 375°F.

Sprinkle top of bread with remaining ½ cup cheese. Continue baking until loaf is golden brown, cheese melts and bread sounds hollow when tapped on bottom, about 10 minutes. Transfer to rack and cool. *(Can be prepared 1 day ahead. Store airtight at room temperature.)*

MAPLE-CINNAMON CAKE

6 SERVINGS

	Nonstick vegetable oil spray
½	cup unsweetened applesauce
½	cup pure maple syrup
¼	cup vegetable oil
1	large egg
1	teaspoon vanilla extract
1½	cups cake flour
½	cup (packed) golden brown sugar
1	teaspoon baking powder
½	teaspoon ground cinnamon
¼	teaspoon baking soda
¼	teaspoon salt

Preheat oven to 400°F. Spray 8 x 8 x 2-inch baking pan with vegetable oil spray. Whisk applesauce, syrup, oil, egg and vanilla in large bowl until blended. Sift flour, brown sugar, baking powder, cinnamon, baking soda and salt into applesauce mixture. Stir to blend. Transfer batter to prepared pan. Bake cake until edges pull away from sides of pan and tester inserted into center comes out clean, about 28 minutes. Transfer pan to rack and cool cake completely. *(Can be prepared 1 day ahead. Cover with plastic and let stand at room temperature.)* Cut into 6 pieces. Wrap each in plastic to transport.

COLD BAKED CHICKEN WITH
BARBECUE SAUCE

SWEET-AND-SOUR COLESLAW

LIGHT AND CREAMY
POTATO SALAD

ICED TEA OR LEMONADE

TRIPLE-BERRY PIE

Menu for Six

*I*t is, quite simply, one of the great old-fashioned pleasures: picking berries from a tangle of bushes, nibbling as you go, slowly, slowly filling the bin as the sun passes by. Once the picking's done, it becomes easy to predict the future: There will be pie for dessert sometime soon. It's practically a law of nature, as natural as sun, rain and scratches after a long day in the brambles.

But first you and yours need sustenance to finish the job—fuel in the form of lunch. So pack up the dishes here and enjoy them right there among the blueberries, strawberries or raspberries, saving the pie recipe (a classic, lattice-topped beauty) to make at home later in the day. Leading up to that berry finale is a menu of delicious cold baked chicken with a sweet and spicy glaze, mixed-cabbage coleslaw and yogurt-based (read low-calorie and low-fat) potato salad with mustard and tarragon flavorings (make them all ahead and refrigerate).

To find out where and when the picking's ripe, check with your local tourism office, agricultural organization or newspaper. Set aside a day, then rise early to pack up a big wicker basket, being sure to include something to sit on, plates, napkins, flatware and glasses, along with plenty of iced tea or lemonade for the thirsty—and pleasurable—work ahead.

COLD BAKED CHICKEN WITH BARBECUE SAUCE

THE HOMEMADE barbecue sauce here takes less than 15 minutes to make and tastes much better than store-bought. Try it on steaks, too.

6 SERVINGS

¾	cup bottled chili sauce
¾	cup ketchup
3	tablespoons dark brown sugar
3	tablespoons cider vinegar
3	garlic cloves, finely chopped
6	large skinless boneless chicken breast halves (about 5 ounces each)

Bring first 5 ingredients to simmer in heavy medium saucepan over low heat. Simmer until reduced to 1 cup, stirring frequently, about 10 minutes. Remove from heat. Season barbecue sauce to taste with pepper.

Preheat oven to 400°F. Line baking sheet with heavy-duty aluminum foil, folding up sides slightly to form rim. Brush both sides of chicken with barbecue sauce. Place chicken on prepared baking sheet. Bake chicken until cooked through, about 18 minutes. Cool 30 minutes. Cover and refrigerate until well chilled. *(Can be prepared 1 day ahead. Keep refrigerated.)* Cut chicken crosswise into ½-inch-thick slices. Transport in plastic container; keep chilled.

SWEET-AND-SOUR COLESLAW

6 SERVINGS

½	cup cider vinegar
¼	cup plus 2 tablespoons apple juice
3	tablespoons vegetable oil
2	small garlic cloves, minced
1½	teaspoons sugar
¾	teaspoon salt
6	cups finely shredded red cabbage
6	cups finely shredded green cabbage
1½	large carrots, coarsely shredded
¼	cup plus 2 tablespoons finely chopped fresh parsley

Whisk vinegar, juice, oil, garlic, sugar and salt in large bowl to blend. Add remaining ingredients and toss well to mix. Season with pepper. Cover and refrigerate until cold, tossing occasionally, about 2 hours for crisp slaw. *(Can be prepared 8 hours ahead; slaw will soften.)* Transport in plastic container; keep chilled.

LIGHT AND CREAMY POTATO SALAD

6 SERVINGS

2	pounds small red-skinned potatoes
1½	cups plain low-fat yogurt
3	tablespoons country-style Dijon mustard
3	tablespoons finely chopped fresh tarragon
1	green or red bell pepper, cut into matchstick-size strips

⅔ cup thinly sliced green onions

⅔ cup thinly sliced celery

Cook potatoes in medium saucepan of boiling salted water until tender, about 25 minutes. Drain and cool. Cut potatoes into quarters.

Whisk yogurt, mustard and tarragon in large bowl until blended. Add potatoes, bell pepper, green onions and celery and toss. Season with salt and pepper. Cover and chill well, about 3 hours. *(Can be prepared 1 day ahead.)* Transport in plastic container; keep chilled.

TRIPLE-BERRY PIE

6 SERVINGS

PASTRY

  2 cups all purpose flour

  2 tablespoons sugar

  ¾ teaspoon salt

  ½ cup chilled solid vegetable shortening, cut into pieces

  ¼ cup (½ stick) chilled unsalted butter, cut into pieces

  4 tablespoons (about) cold water

FILLING

  1 1-pint basket blueberries

  2 1-pint baskets strawberries, hulled, halved

  1 ½-pint basket raspberries

  ¾ cup plus 1 tablespoon sugar

  ¼ cup quick-cooking tapioca

  1 egg, beaten to blend (for glaze)

FOR PASTRY: Mix first 3 ingredients in processor. Add shortening and butter and cut in using on/off turns until mixture resembles coarse meal. Add enough water by tablespoonfuls until dough just begins to clump together. Gather dough into ball; divide in half. Flatten each piece into disk. Wrap in plastic and chill 1 hour.

Preheat oven to 375°F. Roll out 1 dough piece on floured surface to 13-inch round. Transfer to 9-inch glass pie dish. Trim and crimp edges. Freeze 15 minutes. Line with foil. Fill with pie weights or dried beans. Bake until edges are golden, 20 minutes. Remove foil and weights. Cool crust. Maintain oven temperature. Roll out remaining dough piece on floured surface to 13-inch round. Cut out ½-inch-wide strips.

FOR FILLING: Toss berries, ¾ cup sugar and tapioca in large bowl. Let stand 20 minutes.

Mound filling in crust. Place dough strips atop pie, forming lattice; trim excess. Gently press edges to adhere to crust. Brush with egg glaze. Top with 1 tablespoon sugar. Bake until crust is golden and filling bubbles at edges, about 40 minutes. Cool. *(Can be made 1 day ahead. Store airtight at room temperature.)*

BIKE TRIP PICNIC

STEAK SANDWICH WITH
AVOCADO SALSA

CUCUMBER, ORANGE AND
RADISH SALAD

JICAMA-HOMINY-POTATO SALAD

MEXICAN BEER OR BOTTLED WATER

CHOCOLATE CHUNK COOKIES
WITH WALNUTS

Menu for Six

Those traveling on foot see a small area very well; motorists see a large area not so well. Bicyclists, however, get the best of both worlds: They pass through the landscape at a rate that keeps interest high while traveling slowly enough to be able to see the small pond hidden off the side of the road or to rest awhile on that grassy slope that has a view of the distant sea—no parking spot required. Being on a bicycle with some wonderful food along for the ride is surely one definition of freedom.

Pack this menu in your panniers, and when you and the gang stop for lunch, you'll be rewarded for your efforts to that point and satisfied, energized and revitalized for the ride home. Wedges of a big steak sandwich layered with roasted red peppers, avocado salsa and Jack cheese get this southwestern-flavored picnic off to a tasty start. Two crisp and refreshing salads, one with cucumber, oranges, radishes and cilantro, the other with potatoes, jicama and hominy, keep the theme going. Make everything ahead and hand everyone their own load to carry.

And don't forget to add two or three of the impressively sized chocolate-chunk, walnut-studded spice cookies to those lunch bags. They will make that final pedal up the hill possible. Because once you get there, your little slice of bicycle-luncheon paradise may seem like the grandest dining room in the entire world.

STEAK SANDWICH WITH AVOCADO SALSA

6 SERVINGS

¼	cup plus 1 tablespoon olive oil
2	large garlic cloves, minced
2	teaspoons dried oregano
2	teaspoons ground cumin
1	2-pound flank steak
2	firm but ripe avocados, pitted, peeled, chopped
1	16-ounce container thick chunky salsa, well drained
1	10- to 12-inch round loaf sourdough bread
2	7-ounce jars roasted red peppers, drained, thinly sliced
7	ounces thinly sliced Monterey Jack cheese

Prepare barbecue (medium-high heat) or preheat broiler. Combine ¼ cup olive oil, garlic, oregano and cumin in small bowl. Rub mixture over both sides of steak. Sprinkle steak with salt and pepper. Grill or broil to desired doneness, about 5 minutes per side for medium-rare. Transfer steak to work surface. Cool. Cut steak across grain into thin strips.

Toss chopped avocados with salsa in medium bowl. Season to taste with salt and pepper.

Using serrated knife, split bread loaf in half horizontally. Scoop out bread from center of each half, leaving 1-inch-thick layer of bread and crust intact. Brush cut surfaces of bread with remaining 1 tablespoon olive oil. Arrange steak slices in hollow of bottom half of bread. Arrange red peppers over steak. Arrange cheese over peppers. Spoon avocado salsa over cheese. Top with second half of bread. Wrap sandwich in foil and refrigerate at least 4 hours and up to 8 hours.

Cut into wedges. Wrap in plastic to transport.

CUCUMBER, ORANGE AND RADISH SALAD

6 SERVINGS

6	oranges
6	tablespoons canola oil
3	tablespoons white wine vinegar
1	tablespoon grated orange peel
1½	teaspoons ground cumin
⅜	teaspoon cayenne pepper
3	cucumbers, peeled, halved lengthwise, sliced
18	radishes, thinly sliced
6	tablespoons chopped fresh cilantro

Cut off peel and white pith from oranges. Slice oranges into rounds. Cut each round crosswise in half. Whisk oil, vinegar, orange peel, cumin and cayenne in large bowl. Add oranges, cucumbers, radishes and cilantro; toss to coat. Season to taste with salt. *(Can be made 6 hours ahead. Cover and chill.)* Transport in plastic container.

JICAMA-HOMINY-POTATO SALAD

6 SERVINGS

½ cup olive oil

6 tablespoons fresh lime juice

3 large garlic cloves, peeled

2 tablespoons chopped jalapeño chilies

3½ teaspoons ground cumin

1 teaspoon dried oregano

1 15-ounce can golden hominy, drained

¾ cup chopped fresh cilantro

⅔ cup diced peeled jicama

½ cup chopped white onion

2 pounds medium-large Yukon Gold potatoes (about 6), unpeeled

Puree first 6 ingredients in blender until almost smooth. Season generously with salt. Pour into medium bowl. Mix in hominy, ½ cup cilantro, jicama and onion. Let stand for 30 minutes.

Steam potatoes until tender, about 30 minutes. Cool 15 minutes; peel. Cut lengthwise in half, then crosswise into ½-inch-thick slices. Place in large bowl. Add hominy mixture and toss to blend. Season to taste with salt and pepper. Sprinkle with remaining ¼ cup cilantro. *(Can be made 6 hours ahead. Cover; let stand at room temperature.)* Transport in plastic container.

CHOCOLATE CHUNK COOKIES WITH WALNUTS

MAKES ABOUT 24

¾ cup (1½ sticks) unsalted butter, room temperature

½ cup (packed) golden brown sugar

⅓ cup sugar

1 large egg

1 teaspoon vanilla extract

1⅔ cups all purpose flour

1 teaspoon salt

1 teaspoon ground ginger

1 teaspoon ground cinnamon

½ teaspoon baking soda

14 ounces semisweet chocolate, coarsely chopped

1 cup coarsely chopped toasted walnuts

Powdered sugar

Beat first 3 ingredients in large bowl until light and fluffy. Add egg and vanilla and beat until blended. Sift flour, salt, ginger, cinnamon and baking soda into butter mixture. Beat until blended. Stir in chocolate and walnuts. Refrigerate dough until firm, about 1 hour.

Preheat oven to 350°F. Line 2 heavy large baking sheets with parchment paper. Form dough into balls, using generous tablespoon for each. Place on sheets, spacing 2 inches apart.

Bake cookies until golden brown, about 18 minutes. Transfer baking sheets to racks. Cool 5 minutes. Transfer cookies to racks and cool completely. Sprinkle with powdered sugar. *(Can be prepared ahead. Store in airtight container at room temperature 2 days or freeze up to 2 weeks.)* Wrap in plastic to transport.

CRUSTY BREAD WITH GRAPES
AND CHEESE

FRITTATA WITH MUSTARD GREENS
AND FONTINA

TOMATOES VINAIGRETTE

PINOT GRIGIO

QUICK TIRAMISÙ

Menu for Two

Sometimes it's nice simply to stop, pull back and take a day off for just you and the one you love best. Here's an idea: Pick a Saturday on the calendar and plan nothing else. Turn the kids over to their grandparents and invite your loved one out for a slow, lazy day of relaxing together, lying in the shade on a blanket, sipping wine, eating good food, getting to know each other again.

Keep it simple, keep it easy. Romance abhors daunting tasks, and this little menu has none. You can prepare the main course and the salad in the morning, together, one of you sautéing the mustard greens for the cheesy frittata (a quiche-like dish, minus the crust), the other whipping up the dressing for the tomatoes vinaigrette. Both are great at room temperature. The individual tiramisù desserts, which taste rich and complex even though they're fast and simple to make, can be done a day in advance and brought along in a cooler. Pack everything else, including some grapes and cheese and a freshly baked baguette, in a picnic basket with all the necessary implements (you won't need much; remember, for once it's just you two) and pick up a bottle of wine (don't forget the opener and glasses). Now put the top down on the convertible and go. (Romance loves convertibles.)

FRITTATA WITH MUSTARD GREENS AND FONTINA

SLICES OF THIS "crustless quiche" are an elegant alternative to sandwiches. Grapes, a soft-ripened cheese and bread or crackers make an elegant and easy start to the picnic.

2 SERVINGS

2	tablespoons olive oil
1	small bunch mustard greens, stems trimmed, leaves cut into 1-inch-wide strips
1	tablespoon finely chopped garlic
4	large eggs, beaten to blend
½	cup diced Fontina cheese

Preheat broiler. Heat oil in medium broilerproof skillet over medium-high heat. Add greens; stir until wilted and tender, about 2 minutes. Add garlic; stir 1 minute. Sprinkle generously with salt and pepper. Pour eggs over greens; stir to blend. Sprinkle with cheese. Cover skillet; cook until frittata is almost set but top is still runny, about 2 minutes. Place skillet under broiler. Broil until top is set and cheese bubbles, about 1 minute. Cut around frittata to loosen. Slide out onto plate. *(Can be prepared 8 hours ahead. Cool; wrap in plastic and refrigerate.)* Cut into wedges. Wrap in plastic to transport.

TOMATOES VINAIGRETTE

IF YOU LIKE, serve this chopped salad with slices of French bread baguette.

2 SERVINGS

2	medium tomatoes, chopped
2	tablespoons red wine vinegar
1	small garlic clove, finely chopped
¼	teaspoon salt
¼	teaspoon dried oregano
	Pinch of sugar
1	tablespoon olive oil (optional)
1	tablespoon chopped fresh Italian parsley

Combine first 6 ingredients in medium bowl. Mix in oil, if desired. Sprinkle with chopped parsley. Season with pepper. *(Can be prepared 4 hours ahead. Cover and refrigerate.)* Transport salad in plastic container.

QUICK TIRAMISÙ

So QUICK, SO EASY and so good. These are made in individual dishes, which pack up easily. (Lovely goblets would be an option if you're staying home, another time.)

2 SERVINGS

- 6 tablespoons Kahlúa or other coffee liqueur
- 3 tablespoons sugar
- 1 tablespoon water
- 2 teaspoons instant espresso powder or instant coffee powder
- ½ cup whipped cream cheese
- 2 tablespoons whipping cream
- 6 ½-inch-thick slices purchased pound cake
- 2 teaspoons unsweetened cocoa powder

Combine Kahlúa, 1 tablespoon sugar, 1 table-spoon water and instant espresso powder in small bowl; stir until espresso powder dissolves. Combine cream cheese, cream, 1 tablespoon Kahlúa mixture and 2 tablespoons sugar in another small bowl and whisk to blend.

Dip 3 cake slices in Kahlúa mixture; turn to coat. Place 1½ slices of cake in each of two 1¼-cup ramekins. Press gently with fingertips to reach edges of ramekins. Spread half of cheese mixture over cake slices in each ramekin. Dip remaining 3 cake slices in Kahlúa mixture, turning to coat. Top each ramekin with 1½ slices cake, pressing to fit. Sift cocoa over. Cover and refrigerate up to 1 day. Transport in cooler.

SETTING THE SCENE

As if it weren't romantic enough to begin with, a picnic can be made even more appealing in all sorts of ways. First of all, pick the spot carefully. You'll want shade, but make sure the ground isn't damp. Look for something that you can lean against, like a big tree, a stone wall or a large rock. A view is a plus, but it's also nice to be next to a river or a lake, or on the beach.

If you don't have far to walk, bring some of the comforts of home, including a blanket or a sheet to cover the ground, as well as pillows or cushions to lounge on. For a picnic in grand style, pack along wineglasses and proper plates, as well as serving pieces for the food. A portable stereo and several baroque CDs might add to the mood as well.

A picnic under the stars can't be beat when it comes to romantic settings. You might want to choose a familiar spot if there's only the moon to guide your way (lanterns, oil lamps and flashlights can make the going easier too). A trek into your own back yard may be all the adventure you had in mind after dark, but don't rule out public parks, museum grounds, roadside turnoffs or the local beach. All have scene-setting potential. And don't forget the extra sweaters and blankets to ward off the night's chill—and make things cozy.

SMOKED-FISH PÂTÉ WITH PITA CHIPS

TURKEY, BRIE AND PEPERONCINI
SANDWICHES

GREEN BEAN, CORN AND
TOMATO SALAD

SAUVIGNON BLANC OR BEER

FRESH FRUIT

LEMON BISCOTTI

Menu for Six

*T*o call a tailgate party a picnic is, it has to be said, a bit of a stretch. After all, a picnic can usually fit in a basket, but a *tailgate* picnic can fill a car. Bringing along extra stuff is all done in the interest of providing the kind of creature comforts that we tend to associate more with dens than with parking lots. Chairs, camp stoves, coolers, folding tables, ice buckets, tiki torches, CD players, televisions, dance floors—you name it, some wizened tailgater somewhere has toted it along—to the ball game, to the concert, to the beach, to a picnic table by a stream.

Of course, the one thing every tailgate party needs is good food. This menu will keep the folks in the next parking space straining their necks to see just what you're eating. It starts with a delicious smoked-fish pâté served with garlicky baked pita bread wedges. Brie, sliced tomatoes, fresh spinach and *peperoncini* pep up turkey sandwiches served on crusty baguettes, and a green bean, corn and tomato salad goes with them. For dessert, fresh fruit (any seasonal mix will do) is all that's needed with the bake-ahead, lemon-flavored biscotti, which, as it happens, would be perfect with a cup of freshly brewed espresso.

Hey, this is tailgating—you *did* bring the espresso machine, right?

SMOKED-FISH PÂTÉ WITH PITA CHIPS

THE PÂTÉ SHOULD be placed in an airtight container and transported in a cooler. The pita chips can travel in the picnic basket.

6 SERVINGS

4	pita bread rounds, each cut into 8 wedges
3	tablespoons olive oil
	Garlic salt
1	pound smoked fish (such as bluefish, trout or chub), skinned, boned, chopped
½	cup chopped green onions
¼	cup fresh lemon juice
¼	cup cream cheese, room temperature

Preheat oven to 350°F. Place pita wedges on baking sheet. Brush with olive oil. Season with garlic salt. Bake pita until crisp, 7 minutes.

Mix fish, green onions, lemon juice and cream cheese in medium bowl to blend. Spoon pâté into bowl. (*Pita chips and pâté can be prepared 1 day ahead. Store chips in airtight container at room temperature. Cover and refrigerate pâté.*) Place pâté on platter. Surround with pita chips.

TURKEY, BRIE AND PEPERONCINI SANDWICHES

NOT YOUR TYPICAL turkey sandwiches, these include Brie cheese, tomatoes, spinach and *peperoncini* for a terrific mix of flavors.

6 SERVINGS

6	tablespoons Dijon mustard
6	tablespoons mayonnaise
2	tablespoons chopped fresh oregano
2	16-inch-long French bread baguettes
12	ounces Brie, sliced, room temperature
1	pound smoked turkey, thinly sliced
3	large tomatoes, thinly sliced
20	fresh spinach leaves
12	peperoncini, halved lengthwise

Mix first 3 ingredients in small bowl. Cut each baguette lengthwise in half. Spread mustard mixture onto cut sides of baguettes. Top bottom halves of baguettes with cheese, spreading gently. Cover with turkey, tomatoes, spinach and peperoncini, dividing equally. Sprinkle with salt and pepper. Cover with tops of baguettes. Cut each baguette diagonally into 6 sandwiches. (*Sandwiches can be prepared 6 hours ahead. Wrap tightly in foil and refrigerate.*) Transport in cooler.

GREEN BEAN, CORN AND TOMATO SALAD

MAKE THIS COLORFUL salad the night before the picnic, if you like.

6 SERVINGS

6	ounces green beans, cut into 1-inch lengths
3	ears white corn, kernels removed
½	cup white wine vinegar
6	tablespoons vegetable oil
5	tablespoons sugar
3	large tomatoes, chopped
½	cup chopped red onion
⅓	cup chopped fresh parsley

Cook beans in large saucepan of boiling salted water 2 minutes. Add corn kernels and cook until vegetables are crisp-tender, about 2 minutes longer. Drain well.

Whisk vinegar, oil and sugar in large bowl to blend. Season with salt and pepper. Add beans, corn, tomatoes, onion and parsley; toss to coat. Season with salt and pepper. Cover; chill at least 2 hours or overnight. Transport in plastic container in cooler. If desired, drain excess dressing from salad before serving.

LEMON BISCOTTI

SERVE WITH A seasonal mix of fresh fruits.

MAKES ABOUT 3½ DOZEN

2¼	cups all purpose flour
½	cup chopped toasted almonds
1	teaspoon baking powder
½	teaspoon salt
1	cup sugar
½	cup (1 stick) unsalted butter, room temperature
2	large eggs
¼	cup fresh lemon juice
1	tablespoon grated lemon peel
1	teaspoon vanilla extract
½	teaspoon almond extract
1	large egg white, beaten to blend (for glaze)

Preheat oven to 350°F. Spray heavy large baking sheet with nonstick spray. Mix flour and next 3 ingredients in medium bowl. Beat sugar and butter in large bowl until light. Add eggs 1 at a time, beating well after each addition. Beat in juice, peel and extracts. Mix in dry ingredients.

Turn dough out onto heavily floured surface. Divide in half. Shape each dough half into 11-inch-long log. Place on baking sheet, spacing 4 inches apart. Flatten each log to width of 1¾ inches. Brush with egg white. Bake until pale golden, about 30 minutes. Transfer to work surface; cool. Maintain oven temperature.

Cut each log crosswise on diagonal into ⅓-inch-thick slices. Place cookies cut side down on baking sheet. Bake until golden, turning once, about 20 minutes. Transfer cookies to racks; cool. (Can be made ahead. Store airtight at room temperature 1 week or freeze 1 month.)

SANGRIA WITH APPLE AND ORANGE

CHIVE-GOAT CHEESE SPREAD

CHICKEN BROCHETTES WITH
CRAB APPLE JELLY MARINADE

SKEWERED VEGETABLES WITH
BASIL BUTTER

WILD RICE, APRICOT AND
ALMOND SALAD

CHOCOLATE-CHERRY TRUFFLE TART

Menu for Eight

What's better than spending a lazy summer day by a lake? Extending the pleasures of the day into the night with a relaxing sunset dinner at the water's edge. (Of course, you *could* wait until everyone else has had their day's fun and roll up to the lake in the late afternoon, just as things are quieting down.)

The food in this menu is elegant without being fussy, the kind of picnic that can bring a certain sophistication to a casual setting. Choose a site that has barbecues or bring your own (don't forget the charcoal, tongs, kitchen mitt and matches), as both the chicken brochettes and the vegetable skewers are best hot off the grill. A turn over the fire is all that's required, though, since the brochettes are transported in their marinade and the skewers are threaded and ready to cook, with a make-ahead basil butter for extra flavor. A delicious wild rice salad with dried apricots, currants and almonds rounds out the plate (and transports in a plastic container in a cooler). To get a slow start on the evening, unpack the chive-flavored goat cheese spread and French bread, and fill glasses with the apple and orange sangria.

As the light fades over the water after dinner, you and your guests can dig into the sinful chocolate-cherry truffle-like tart—so good it can hold its own with the breathtaking sunset view.

SANGRIA WITH APPLE AND ORANGE

8 SERVINGS

2	750-ml bottles Beaujolais or Zinfandel wine
3	cups cranberry-apple juice cocktail
1	cup orange juice
1	cup sugar
1	small apple, cored, sliced
2	oranges, each cut into 8 rounds
	Ice cubes

Combine first 4 ingredients in large thermos. Stir until sugar dissolves. Add apple and half of orange slices. Refrigerate until well chilled, at least 2 hours and up to 8 hours.

Fill 8 glasses with ice. Pour sangria over. Garnish rim of each glass with orange slice.

CHIVE-GOAT CHEESE SPREAD

MAKING THIS at least a day ahead will allow the flavors to blend. In addition to the cheese shape described here, you can form the mixture into a square, a pyramid or an oblong roll, covering them with everything from herbs to cracked peppercorns.

8 SERVINGS

8	ounces soft fresh goat cheese (such as Montrachet), room temperature
4	ounces cream cheese, room temperature
6	tablespoons minced fresh chives (about 1 ounce)
1	garlic clove, pressed
12	whole long fresh chives
1	French bread baguette, sliced

Combine goat cheese, cream cheese, minced chives and garlic in medium bowl. Stir with fork until well blended. Place large piece of plastic wrap on work surface. Arrange whole chives in crisscross pattern atop center of plastic. Spoon cheese mixture into center of chives, forming 4- to 5-inch round. Lift edges of plastic, wrapping chives around cheese and covering cheese completely. Refrigerate overnight. *(Can be prepared 2 days ahead. Keep refrigerated.)* Transport in cooler; serve with baguette slices.

CHICKEN BROCHETTES WITH CRAB APPLE JELLY MARINADE

THIS RECIPE REQUIRES a grill, so if there isn't one where you're going, consider packing up a portable one. The jelly in the marinade gives a nice glaze to the chicken as it grills.

8 SERVINGS

1	12-ounce jar crab apple jelly or apricot jelly
¼	cup extra-virgin olive oil
¼	cup vegetable oil
2	tablespoons minced garlic
8	skinless boneless chicken breast halves, each cut crosswise into 4 strips
8	10- to 12-inch bamboo skewers, soaked in water 30 minutes

Stir crab apple jelly in heavy medium saucepan over medium heat until melted. Whisk in olive oil, vegetable oil and garlic. Cool marinade.

Thread 4 chicken pieces on each skewer. Place skewers in baking pan. Sprinkle chicken with salt and pepper. Set aside ¼ cup marinade. Brush remaining marinade over chicken. Cover chicken and reserved ¼ cup marinade separately and refrigerate at least 2 hours and up to 8 hours. Transport chicken skewers and remaining marinade in cooler.

Prepare barbecue (medium-high heat). Grill chicken until cooked through, basting frequently with marinade in baking pan, about 10 minutes. Brush reserved ¼ cup marinade over chicken and serve.

SKEWERED VEGETABLES WITH BASIL BUTTER

THESE PRETTY VEGETABLE skewers can be assembled up to eight hours before grilling.

8 SERVINGS

¾	cup (1½ sticks) butter, room temperature
6	tablespoons fresh lemon juice
2	tablespoons minced garlic
2	tablespoons minced fresh basil or 2 teaspoons dried
16	small red-skinned potatoes
1	large onion, cut into sixteen 1-inch chunks
1½	yellow bell peppers, cut into sixteen 1-inch pieces
3	zucchini, cut into sixteen 1-inch-thick rounds
3	ears corn, shucked, cut into sixteen 1-inch-thick rounds
16	10- to 12-inch bamboo skewers, soaked in water 30 minutes

Mix first 4 ingredients in small bowl. *(Basil butter can be prepared 2 days ahead. Cover and refrigerate. Bring to room temperature before using.)*

Cook potatoes in large saucepan of boiling salted water until just tender, about 10 minutes. Drain and cool. Thread 1 piece of each vegetable on each skewer. *(Can be prepared 8 hours ahead. Cover skewers and refrigerate.)* Transport basil butter and skewers in cooler.

Prepare barbecue (medium-high heat). Grill all vegetables until lightly charred and crisp-tender, brushing frequently with basil butter and turning often, about 10 minutes. Season to taste with salt and pepper and serve.

WILD RICE, APRICOT AND ALMOND SALAD

DRIED APRICOTS AND currants add a touch of sweetness to this delicious salad.

8 SERVINGS

6 14½-ounce cans low-salt chicken broth

2 cups wild rice (about 12 ounces)

1 cup dried apricots (about 6 ounces), coarsely chopped

½ cup dried currants

1 cup blanched slivered almonds, toasted

⅔ cup chopped red onion

½ cup chopped fresh parsley

6 tablespoons tarragon vinegar

4 teaspoons Dijon mustard

2 garlic cloves, minced

1 cup olive oil

Bring chicken broth to boil in heavy large saucepan. Mix in wild rice. Reduce heat to medium-low. Simmer uncovered until rice is tender, stirring occasionally, about 50 minutes. Drain rice well. Transfer rice to bowl. Mix in dried apricots and currants. Cool completely.

Mix almonds, onion and parsley into rice. Whisk vinegar, mustard and garlic in small bowl. Gradually whisk in olive oil. Mix enough dressing into salad to season to taste. Season with salt and pepper. *(Can be prepared 1 day ahead. Cover with plastic wrap and refrigerate.)* Transport salad in plastic container.

CHOCOLATE-CHERRY TRUFFLE TART

THIS INDULGENCE is simple to make and can be prepared a day ahead of time.

8 SERVINGS

1 Tart Crust (see recipe opposite)

1 cup cherry preserves (about one 12-ounce jar)

2 tablespoons water

⅓ cup whipping cream

2 tablespoons (¼ stick) unsalted butter

4 ounces bittersweet (not unsweetened) or semisweet chocolate, finely chopped

1¼ pounds fresh Bing cherries, pitted, halved

Fresh mint sprigs

Preheat oven to 350°F. Roll out Tart Crust dough on lightly floured work surface to 13 x 10-inch rectangle. Transfer to 11 x 8-inch rectangular tart pan with removable bottom, pressing firmly. Fold overhang in; press, forming double-thick sides. Freeze 15 minutes.

Line crust with foil. Fill with dried beans or pie weights. Bake until sides are set, about 15 minutes. Remove foil and beans. Bake until crust is golden brown and baked through, piercing with fork if crust bubbles, about 15 minutes. Transfer pan to rack and cool crust.

Combine preserves and 2 tablespoons water in heavy small saucepan. Stir over low heat until preserves melt. Strain into medium bowl, pressing firmly on solids to extract liquid. Discard any solids in strainer.

Combine cream, butter and ¼ cup preserve mixture in heavy medium saucepan. Stir over low heat until butter melts. Add chocolate and stir until chocolate melts and mixture is smooth. Remove from heat. Cool 15 minutes.

Spread chocolate mixture evenly in bottom of crust. Chill until almost set, 20 minutes.

Arrange cherries decoratively over chocolate, pressing slightly to adhere. Rewarm remaining preserve mixture over low heat. Brush generously over cherries. Chill until chocolate sets, about 1 hour. *(Can be made 1 day ahead. Cover and keep chilled.)* Transport in covered container in cooler.

Garnish tart with mint and serve.

TART CRUST

MAKES 1 CRUST

1¼	cups all purpose flour
⅓	cup powdered sugar
½	teaspoon salt
10	tablespoons (1¼ sticks) chilled unsalted butter, cut into pieces
2	large egg yolks
1	tablespoon cold water

Mix flour, powdered sugar and salt in processor. Add butter; process until mixture resembles coarse meal. Mix egg yolks and 1 tablespoon water in small bowl. Add to flour mixture and process until moist clumps form.

Gather dough into ball; flatten into square. Wrap in plastic and refrigerate 1 hour. *(Can be prepared 3 days ahead. Keep refrigerated. Let dough soften briefly at room temperature before rolling out.)*

PACKING A PICNIC

There's no reason to find yourself in some gorgeous setting (at the edge of a still lake at sunset, for example) eating soggy sandwiches and crumbled cookies. If you take the time to pack the food and other items carefully, your picnic will go much more smoothly.

For efficiency's sake, pack your basket in reverse order of the meal, with dessert on the bottom (in a sturdy plastic container), topped with the main course, then any salads, rolls and condiments, followed by crudités, chips and other starters. If there is too much to fit in one basket, organize things logically, with all the plates, glasses, linens and cutlery together, the starters in another container, and so on.

Food that needs to be kept cold should be packed in a cooler unless your picnic spot isn't far from your kitchen. Use ice or gel-filled freezer packs (keep these in your freezer for spur-of-the-moment picnics). Plastic containers with tight lids are essential. Screw on any lids as tightly as possible; to be extra-safe, pack jars in zipper-locking plastic bags.

Anything breakable, such as jars, glasses, plates, and bottles, should be wrapped in dishcloths or thick napkins, then placed near the top of the basket. Take a separate bag for trash and small plastic bags and aluminum foil for leftovers. Another bag could hold sunscreen, bug spray, hand soap, and wet wipes.

Menu for Twelve

They are the summer days everyone looks forward to all year long, days at the beach that begin early and stretch into the night with sweatshirts, a big fire and good food. They are the days every child remembers, chronicled in school reports and archived in family photo albums.

With a few advance preparations, this time-honored cookout can be easier than ever. The menu pays tribute to some favorites while adding a few twists to make them better than you remember.

Lemonade is one of the best warm-weather refreshers; freshly squeezed lemonade enlivened with sprigs of fresh mint is even better (pack a cooler of beer, too). Good old hot dogs are fine, but unusually flavored sausages in homemade onion buns are better still (pick up a selection of sausages for the adults; the kids will want the familiar).

While the fire is heating up, pass around the dill-scented dip with crudités and chips. Two make-head salads, one a vegetable and garbanzo bean combo, the other a mix of fruit in a carved watermelon "basket" (complete with step-by-step instructions, in case you always wanted to know how to make one), go with the sausages and dogs. And for dessert, there are updated and kid-friendly s'mores. A word of advice: Bring along enough for the grown-ups, too.

32-LEMON-ADE

GOOD OLD-FASHIONED lemonade, sweetened with sugar and garnished with mint. (Keep this recipe on hand if you have a flourishing lemon tree in your back yard.)

12 SERVINGS

32	large lemons, halved
4	cups cold water
3	cups (about) sugar
	Ice cubes
	Mint sprigs

Squeeze lemon juice into bowl. Strain into large thermos. Add water and 3 cups sugar; stir until sugar dissolves. Add more sugar to taste if desired. Refrigerate until well chilled.

Fill cups with ice. Pour lemonade over. Garnish with mint and serve.

SPICY DILL DIP

THE CLASSIC sour cream dip, made new with a handful of fresh dill, some chili sauce and a hint of garlic. It works equally well with raw vegetables and potato chips.

MAKES ABOUT 2 CUPS

1	cup sour cream
6	tablespoons mayonnaise
¼	cup minced fresh dill or 4 teaspoons dried dillweed
2	tablespoons minced fresh parsley
2	tablespoons minced green onion
2	tablespoons chili sauce
2	garlic cloves, minced
1	teaspoon dry mustard
½	teaspoon Worcestershire sauce
	Carrot sticks
	Sugar snap peas
	Jicama sticks
	Radishes
	Cherry tomatoes
	Cucumber sticks
	Potato chips

Combine first 9 ingredients in medium bowl and blend thoroughly. Season to taste with salt and pepper. Refrigerate until well chilled. Transport in plastic container in cooler.

Serve dip with vegetables and chips.

HOT DOGS AND SAUSAGES IN PEPPER-ONION ROLLS

PEPPERY HOMEMADE rolls give new meaning to "hot dogs at the beach." You can make them ahead and refrigerate or freeze them, but if time gets short, don't hesitate to substitute good store-bought buns. For the adults, bring along a selection of unusually flavored (fully cooked) sausages; for the kids, stick with regular hot dogs. (Don't forget to pack up all your favorite toppings, too.)

MAKES 24

½	cup (1 stick) unsalted butter
2½	cups finely diced yellow onions
2½	cups milk
4	teaspoons sugar
1	envelope dry yeast
4	teaspoons salt
1	tablespoon black pepper
5	cups (about) unbleached all purpose flour
	Grilled sausages and hot dogs

Melt butter in heavy medium skillet over medium heat. Add onions and cook until translucent, stirring occasionally, about 10 minutes. Drain onion mixture in sieve set over medium bowl. Transfer onions to small bowl; reserve drained butter in medium bowl.

Bring milk and sugar to boil in heavy medium saucepan, stirring to dissolve sugar. Cool mixture to 110°F, about 5 minutes. Sprinkle yeast over; stir to dissolve. Let stand until foamy, about 5 minutes. Add to reserved butter; mix in salt and pepper. Stir in enough flour 1 cup at a time to form soft, slightly sticky dough. Turn dough out onto heavily floured surface and knead until smooth, about 5 minutes. Lightly grease large bowl. Add dough, turning to coat. Cover bowl with towel and let dough rise in warm draft-free area until doubled in volume, about 1½ hours.

Lightly butter 2 large baking sheets. Punch dough down. Divide dough in half. Knead each piece on lightly floured surface 2 minutes. Roll 1 piece out on lightly floured surface into 10 x 15-inch rectangle. Cut into two 5 x 15-inch rectangles, using pizza cutter or large knife. Cut each rectangle crosswise into six 5 x 2½-inch-wide strips. Fold each strip lengthwise in half. Press seams to seal. Trim corners of each, rounding slightly. Transfer rolls to prepared sheets, spacing ½ inch apart. Repeat with remaining dough piece, forming 12 more rolls. Cover with towel and let rise in warm draft-free area until puffy, about 1 hour.

Position racks in top and lowest third of oven and preheat to 400°F. Sprinkle onion over rolls. Bake until golden brown, 20 minutes. Cool 5 minutes. Transfer rolls to racks and cool. (*Rolls can be prepared ahead. Seal tightly in plastic bags and refrigerate up to 3 days or freeze up to 1 month.*) Serve with grilled sausages and hot dogs.

VEGETABLE AND GARBANZO BEAN SALAD

HERE'S A FAST and refreshing salad of corn, red bell peppers, celery, garbanzo beans and peas in a creamy dressing.

MAKES ABOUT 12 CUPS

6	large ears of corn, kernels cut from cob
2	red bell peppers, chopped
4	celery stalks, chopped
2	16-ounce cans garbanzo beans (chickpeas), rinsed, drained
2	10-ounce packages frozen peas, thawed, drained
2	bunches green onions, chopped
1	cup mayonnaise
6	tablespoons fresh lemon juice
2	garlic cloves, chopped
1	tablespoon chopped fresh oregano or 1 teaspoon dried
1	tablespoon ground cumin
	Fresh cilantro sprigs

Cook corn kernels in large saucepan of boiling water until just tender, about 5 minutes. Drain well. Transfer to large bowl and cool. Add bell peppers, celery, garbanzo beans, peas and green onions and toss gently. Mix mayonnaise, lemon juice, garlic and oregano in small bowl. Add dressing to bean mixture and toss gently. Season with salt and pepper. Cover and refrigerate until well chilled, about 1 hour. *(Can be prepared 6 hours ahead.)* Sprinkle cumin over. Garnish with cilantro. Transport in plastic container.

FRESH FRUIT SALAD IN WATERMELON BASKET

A COLORFUL MIX of fresh summer fruit fills a decoratively carved watermelon.

12 SERVINGS

3	cups green grapes
3	cups sliced strawberries
3	cups sliced plums
1½	cups sliced peaches
1½	cups orange segments
1½	cups sliced peeled kiwi
¾	cup Grand Marnier or other orange liqueur
¾	cup orange juice
3	tablespoons sugar
1	large watermelon

Combine all ingredients except watermelon in large bowl and toss gently.

Measure from work surface to center of watermelon on each side and each end, scoring each spot with tip of sharp knife. Draw and score line around center, connecting each scored spot. Draw and score shape of handle over top. Cut large *X* on either side of handle to release pressure. Cut through scored lines from one side of handle to halfway mark and around; repeat on other side of handle. Cut away melon to either side of, and under, handle. Scoop out melon with melon baller, leaving 1-inch shell. Add melon to fruit salad. Scallop edges of basket with melon baller. Cover and refrigerate salad and basket up to 8 hours.

Transport in cooler. Fill basket with salad just before serving, refilling as necessary.

WHITE AND MILK CHOCOLATE S'MORES

THE ORIGINAL campfire treat for kids gets dressed up for this barbecue. Half the fun is roasting the marshmallows outdoors, but the end product is just as good when the marshmallows are toasted under the broiler.

12 SERVINGS

24   graham cracker halves

2   3.5-ounce white chocolate candy bars, broken into segments

2   3.5-ounce milk chocolate candy bars, broken into segments

24   large marshmallows

Arrange 12 crackers on platter. Top with white and milk chocolate segments. Thread marshmallows onto skewers; hold over flame until charred. Place 2 marshmallows atop chocolate segments on each cracker. Cover with remaining crackers, pressing gently. Serve hot.

BUILDING AN OUTDOOR FIRE

Beaches, national parks and wilderness areas have different rules and guidelines regarding campfires: Some have designated fire pits; some require the use of metal containers; and some don't allow campfires at all, only camping stoves, which can be purchased at outdoor outfitters. The metal containers resemble buckets and can also usually be bought at outfitters or at general-purpose stores near most wilderness areas.

When it comes to building a fire in a fire pit, which is basically a cleared area of ground within a circle of stones, begin with small pieces of wood and dry debris piled in the shape of a miniature tepee. (Pack in your own firewood and kindling.) As the flames become stronger, add larger pieces of wood until the fire is hot enough to cook your food. Bring a grill rack if possible, which will simplify roasting anything beyond hot dogs and marshmallows.

Afterward, let the fire mostly burn out, then cover the remains with dirt or sand until no embers remain. The idea is to leave the picnic area exactly as you found it—without a trace of your having been there.

GRILLED SWEET-AND-SOUR
PORK

CHILI-CHEESE CORN

ZUCCHINI SALAD WITH
POPPY SEED VINAIGRETTE

BEER AND SODAS

ROCKY ROAD WEDGES

Menu for Eight

Maybe it has to do with sleeping in a tent, or having to walk 20 yards (under a starry sky, mind you) to fetch some water for washing up, or simply having nature so near, but when some people go camping they tend to revert to Stone Age cuisine: Toss some undistin- guished ground meat on the fire, burn it, add a slice of cheese, throw it on a cold bun, team it with potato chips, eat it off a paper plate in the dark and call it dinner.

Clearly, these folks have not been shopping for camping equipment lately. With all that great gear out there, from portable grills to nifty utensils, easy-to-light lanterns to colorful tin plates, it's no more difficult to dine in style at the campsite than it is to "rough it" unnecessarily.

Key to the ease of this menu is prepping things ahead. The main course is pork tenderloins that go into a sweet-and-sour marinade at home, then into a cooler. At the campsite, they cook up in about 20 minutes. Likewise, you can bake the cheesy corn side dish at home and just warm it over the fire in a cast-iron skillet. An easy zucchini salad with a do-ahead dressing requires only a last-minute tossing, and for dessert, just pull the yummy rocky road wedge cookies out of their container, since you've made them the day before.

It's a great dinner: so simple, so stylish—and so non-Neolithic.

GRILLED SWEET-AND-SOUR PORK

PORK TENDERLOINS are marinated in lemon, soy and honey overnight. Pack them in their marinade in a cooler, then grill them at the campsite. Boil the marinade in a skillet on the grill, then serve it alongside the pork.

8 SERVINGS

¾	cup fresh lemon juice
½	cup soy sauce
6	tablespoons honey
2	small shallots, coarsely chopped
2	large garlic cloves, halved
2	bay leaves, crumbled
2	teaspoons salt
2	teaspoons pepper
1	teaspoon dry mustard
½	teaspoon ground ginger
4	12-ounce pork tenderloins

Puree first 10 ingredients in blender. Divide pork tenderloins between 2 large resealable plastic bags. Add half of marinade to each and seal tightly. Turn to coat. Refrigerate pork overnight. Transport in bags in cooler.

Prepare barbecue (medium-high heat). Remove pork from marinade. Transfer marinade to heavy skillet. Grill pork to desired doneness, turning often, 20 minutes for medium.

Meanwhile, boil marinade in skillet on grill until reduced to sauce consistency.

Slice pork. Serve with sauce.

CHILI-CHEESE CORN

BAKE THIS SIDE DISH at home, then rewarm it in a cast-iron skillet at the campsite.

8 SERVINGS

4	cups fresh corn kernels or frozen, thawed, drained
1	cup grated cheddar cheese
1	8-ounce package cream cheese, room temperature
1	7-ounce can diced green chilies
2	teaspoons chili powder
2	teaspoons ground cumin

Preheat oven to 350°F. Butter 1½-quart baking dish. Mix all ingredients in large bowl until well blended. Transfer to prepared dish. Bake until bubbling, about 30 minutes. Cool. Cover and refrigerate up to 1 day. Transport in cooler.

Prepare barbecue (medium-high heat). Transfer corn mixture to cast-iron skillet. Rewarm over grill and then serve.

ZUCCHINI SALAD WITH POPPY SEED VINAIGRETTE

A SIMPLE SWEET-TART vegetable salad to make ahead and have with dinner.

8 SERVINGS

2½	tablespoons balsamic vinegar or red wine vinegar
2	tablespoons orange juice
1	tablespoon poppy seeds
1	teaspoon sugar
½	teaspoon dry mustard
¼	teaspoon salt
½	cup vegetable oil
1	green onion, minced
8	large zucchini, halved lengthwise, thinly sliced crosswise

Whisk first 6 ingredients in small bowl. Gradually whisk in oil. Mix in green onion. *(Can be prepared 1 day ahead. Cover and refrigerate. Rewhisk before using.)* Transport zucchini in plastic bag and dressing in plastic container in cooler. Place zucchini in large bowl. Toss with enough dressing to coat and serve.

ROCKY ROAD WEDGES

CHOCOLATE CHIPS, almonds and marshmallows combine in these chewy, tasty cookies.

MAKES 24

1	cup (2 sticks) unsalted butter, room temperature
1	cup (packed) brown sugar
2	eggs
1¾	cups all purpose flour
¼	cup unsweetened cocoa powder
1	teaspoon baking soda
½	teaspoon salt
3	cups semisweet chocolate chips (about 18 ounces)
1	cup whole almonds, coarsely chopped (about 6 ounces)
1	cup mini marshmallows

Preheat oven to 350°F. Cream butter and sugar in large bowl until fluffy. Beat in eggs. Combine flour, cocoa powder, baking soda and salt in bowl. Stir dry ingredients into butter mixture. Mix in 2 cups chocolate chips and almonds.

Divide dough in half. Pat each half into 8-inch round on 2 ungreased, rimmed baking sheets. Bake until cookies are set but centers are still soft, about 15 minutes. Sprinkle each round with ½ cup mini marshmallows and ½ cup chocolate chips. Bake until marshmallows and chips soften, about 3 minutes. Cool 5 minutes. Cut each round into 12 wedges. Slide off sheet and cool completely on rack. *(Can be prepared 1 day ahead. Store in airtight container at room temperature.)*

CHILLED CUCUMBER SOUP

PICNIC MUFFULETTA

SIX-BEAN SALAD

CHARDONNAY

BLUEBERRY STREUSEL BARS

Menu for Six

A concert picnic, like a tailgate, will likely be consumed under the watchful eyes of neighboring diners. For this reason, fast food from the drive-through might be a tad embarrassing. You'd like the meal to make an impression, both on your guests and on the looky-loos, but you don't want it to be complicated or cumbersome. The balance to aim for is food that is interesting, easy and plentiful (so that your stomach isn't growling at intermission), as well as compact enough to fit in a small, unobtrusive basket, hamper or backpack.

Here's a satisfying, lightweight feast that hits all the right notes. It will easily feed six without bogging you down, and it makes a lovely spread.

To start, an intriguing, low-fat cucumber soup (serve it from a thermos) gets a lift from honey and mint. The New Orleans specialty sandwich *muffuletta* provides main-course ballast. This version combines the traditional olive salad with cold cuts, cheese and roasted peppers in one large loaf, which gets sliced into wedges at the picnic site. To go with the hearty sandwich there is a six-bean salad that is at least twice as good as the average three-bean version. And since the recipe for the wonderful blueberry streusel bars yields plenty of extras, slip seconds for everyone into your picnic basket. You'll know just what to do when the crowd starts yelling "Encore."

CHILLED CUCUMBER SOUP

SIMPLE, YET SURPRISINGLY elegant, this makes a fresh-tasting beginning to the meal.

6 SERVINGS

6	cups chopped peeled seeded cucumbers (about 4 large)
2	cups plain yogurt
1	tablespoon honey
½	teaspoon minced garlic
3	tablespoons chopped fresh mint
	Additional chopped fresh mint

Puree half of each of first 5 ingredients together in blender until smooth. Transfer to bowl. Repeat with remaining half of same 5 ingredients. Season soup to taste with salt and pepper. Cover and chill until cold. *(Can be prepared 1 day ahead. Keep soup refrigerated.)*

Transport in thermos. Ladle soup into bowls. Garnish with additional mint.

PICNIC MUFFULETTA

A GROUP-SIZE version of an Italian cold-cut and olive-salad sandwich popularized in New Orleans. Slice it into wedges at the concert.

6 SERVINGS

1	cup (packed) fresh basil leaves
½	cup olive oil
½	cup pitted Kalamata olives or other brine-cured black olives
¼	cup drained capers
1	tablespoon chopped garlic
1	round 2-pound loaf sourdough or French bread (about 10 inches in diameter)
¾	pound thinly sliced salami
¾	pound thinly sliced provolone cheese
2	7.25-ounce jars roasted red peppers, drained
1	large onion, thinly sliced
6	plum tomatoes, sliced

Blend first 5 ingredients in processor until olives are finely chopped. Season with salt and pepper. *(Can be made 1 day ahead. Cover and chill.)*

Cut bread horizontally in half. Pull or cut out enough interior bread to leave 1½-inch-thick shell. Spread half of olive dressing on cut side of bottom bread shell. Layer with half each of salami, cheese, peppers, onion and tomatoes. Repeat with remaining salami, cheese, peppers, onion and tomatoes. Spread remaining half of olive dressing on cut side of top bread shell; press shell, dressing side down, onto filling. Wrap loaf tightly in plastic and refrigerate at least 1 hour. *(Can be made 1 day ahead. Keep chilled.)* Transport in cooler.

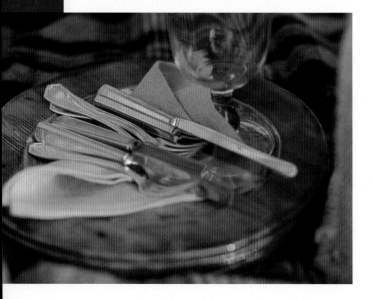

SIX-BEAN SALAD

6 TO 8 SERVINGS

½	pound green beans, trimmed, cut into 2-inch pieces
½	pound yellow wax beans, trimmed, cut into 2-inch pieces
1	small onion, coarsely chopped
½	cup red wine vinegar
½	cup olive oil
1	large garlic clove
3	tablespoons chopped fresh thyme or 3 teaspoons dried
1	15- to 16-ounce can black-eyed peas, rinsed, drained
1	15- to 16-ounce can Great Northern beans, rinsed, drained
1	15- to 16-ounce can kidney beans, rinsed, drained
1½	cups frozen baby lima beans, thawed
	Chopped fresh parsley

Cook green and yellow beans in pot of boiling salted water until crisp-tender, about 4 minutes. Drain. Rinse under cold water; drain again.

Combine onion, vinegar, oil and garlic in blender; puree until smooth. Pour into large bowl. Mix in thyme. Season dressing to taste with salt and pepper. Add black-eyed peas, Great Northern beans, kidney beans and lima beans and toss to blend thoroughly.

Mix green and yellow beans into salad. Cover and chill 4 hours and up to 1 day, tossing occasionally. Sprinkle with parsley. Transport salad in plastic container.

BLUEBERRY STREUSEL BARS

THESE QUICKLY MADE, blueberry-filled bars are wonderfully portable.

MAKES ABOUT 24

CRUST

1½	cups old-fashioned oats
1½	cups all purpose flour
1	cup (packed) golden brown sugar
½	teaspoon baking soda
1	cup (2 sticks) chilled unsalted butter, cut into small pieces

FILLING

1	12-ounce package frozen blueberries, thawed
⅔	cup blueberry or raspberry jam
5	teaspoons all purpose flour
1½	teaspoons minced lemon peel

FOR CRUST: Preheat oven to 375°F. Generously butter 13 x 9 x 2-inch glass baking dish. Combine first 4 ingredients in medium bowl. Add butter; rub with fingertips until mixture resembles coarse meal. Press half of crumb mixture onto bottom of prepared pan. Bake crust until light brown, about 15 minutes. Cool slightly.

FOR FILLING: Mix blueberries, jam, flour and lemon peel in medium bowl.

Spread filling over crust. Sprinkle remaining crumb mixture over. Bake until topping is golden, approximately 35 minutes. Cool in pan. *(Can be prepared 8 hours ahead. Cover; refrigerate or let stand at room temperature.)* Cut into squares and wrap in plastic to transport.

MODERN CLAMBAKE

Now, we know that there are purists out there who will tell you that if this is to be an Authentic Clambake, at least two days of preparation and a full 12 hours at the beach are required, and that only certain types of seaweed, wood and stone will do. Those purists, and the noble culinary legacy they continue, are to be honored indeed. But for anyone who wants to actually stage a clambake rather than just dream about one, we offer this mildly impure, ever-so-slightly adulterated—O.K., not absolutely, entirely authentic but abundantly satisfying, doable and delicious—substitute.

It begins with the premises that you'd rather spend the afternoon lying on the sand than digging a pit in it and that the fresh seafood you've brought along in coolers will taste almost as good cooked over a smoky fire in a barbecue (bring a portable one, or use one of those pits you find on many beaches). The steamed crabs require only a quick warm-up (steam them at home), as does the herb butter, which makes for great dipping. Add a spinach salad (toss the separately packed components), a new-potato salad (ready to eat), a cooler of beer and wine, and homemade strawberry ice cream, and you have the makings of a grand meal. One that won't require any recovery time, either.

OYSTERS AND CLAMS ON THE HALF SHELL

USE WHATEVER shellfish are fresh at your market. Pass plenty of French bread for soaking up the juices and sauces, here and with the other shellfish dishes.

12 SERVINGS

2	dozen fresh oysters
2	dozen fresh clams
	Lemon wedges
	Fresh parsley
	Tangy Cocktail Sauce (see recipe below)

Scrub oysters and clams under running water to remove dirt and grit. Discard any that do not close while being handled. Transport in cooler over crushed ice. Wearing gloves, carefully shuck oysters and clams, cutting muscles attached to upper shells; discard upper shells, leaving shellfish in lower shells. Cut muscles where attached to lower shells. Arrange on platter. Garnish with lemon and parsley. Serve shellfish with Tangy Cocktail Sauce.

TANGY COCKTAIL SAUCE

MAKES ABOUT 3 CUPS

1½	cups ketchup
1	cup chili sauce
¼	cup prepared horseradish
¼	cup fresh lemon juice
2	tablespoons minced fresh basil or 2 teaspoons dried
1	tablespoon minced fresh parsley
2	teaspoons Worcestershire sauce
	Dash of hot pepper sauce

Combine all ingredients in medium bowl. *(Can be prepared 3 days ahead. Cover and refrigerate.)* Transport sauce in cooler.

ROASTED OYSTERS AND CLAMS

A TRUE CLAMBAKE requires an enormous amount of work (see the sidebar on page 187) and a full day at the beach. In this modern interpretation of the feast, the preparations and cooking are simplified. All you need is a barbecue and a supply of fresh-from-the-sea oysters, clams and crabs (transport them in a cooler over crushed ice).

12 SERVINGS

2	cups wood chips, soaked in water 30 minutes, drained
5	dozen fresh oysters, scrubbed
5	dozen fresh clams, scrubbed
	Tangy Cocktail Sauce (see recipe at left)
	Seafood Butter with Herbs (see recipe opposite)

Prepare barbecue (low heat). Place wood chips in 8 x 6-inch foil packet with open top. Set atop coals 5 minutes before grilling shellfish. Arrange oysters and clams directly on barbecue rack. Cover and grill until oysters and clams open, turning occasionally, about 15 minutes for clams and about 20 minutes for oysters (discard any shellfish that do not open).

Remove shellfish from grill using long-handled tongs or oven mitts; transfer to platter. Serve with cocktail sauce and seafood butter.

BEER-STEAMED CRABS

FOR CONVENIENCE, steam the crabs at home and then reheat them on the grill alongside the other shellfish. Be sure to use a very large pot for this recipe or work in batches.

12 SERVINGS

3	cups beer or water
3	cups distilled white vinegar
6	bay leaves, crumbled
6	¼-inch-thick slices peeled fresh ginger
2	tablespoons whole allspice berries
1	tablespoon coriander seeds
1	tablespoon whole black peppercorns
1	teaspoon dried crushed red pepper
1	dozen live Dungeness crabs or 3 dozen small live crabs (such as blue crab)
	Seafood Butter with Herbs (see recipe at right)

Combine beer and vinegar in very large pot. Combine bay leaves, ginger, allspice, coriander, peppercorns and crushed red pepper in small bowl. Stir into beer mixture. Place rack in pot. Add crabs. Cover pot tightly and steam over medium-high heat until crabs are bright red, about 30 minutes. *(Can be prepared 1 day ahead. Cover and refrigerate. Transport cold crabs in cooler. Rewarm crabs over grill until hot, about 10 minutes.)* Transfer crabs to platter. Serve hot or at room temperature with seafood butter.

SEAFOOD BUTTER WITH HERBS

A DELICIOUS SAUCE to serve with cooked shellfish. Don't forget to bring along a small saucepan or skillet to heat it up in.

MAKES ABOUT 3½ CUPS

1½	pounds (6 sticks) butter
8	garlic cloves, minced
½	onion, finely chopped
6	tablespoons minced fresh parsley
¼	cup fresh lemon juice
¼	cup white wine Worcestershire sauce
3	tablespoons minced fresh basil
1	tablespoon minced fresh thyme
	Hot pepper sauce

Melt butter in heavy medium saucepan over low heat. Add next 7 ingredients. Season to taste with hot pepper sauce. *(Can be prepared 4 hours ahead. Transfer to plastic container. Keep at room temperature. Rewarm over low heat before serving.)*

SPINACH SALAD WITH MUSTARD-BACON DRESSING

PREPARE THE DRESSING up to two days ahead. Transport it in a plastic container, then pour over the salad just before serving.

12 SERVINGS

1	pound bacon
1	cup mayonnaise
1	small onion, finely chopped
¼	cup vegetable oil
¼	cup red wine vinegar
3	tablespoons sugar
1	tablespoon Dijon mustard
2	pounds spinach, stemmed, torn into bite-size pieces
1½	pounds mushrooms, sliced
6	hard-boiled eggs, peeled, sliced
½	cup freshly grated Parmesan cheese

Cook bacon in heavy large skillet until crisp. Drain on paper towels; reserve 3 tablespoons drippings for dressing. Crumble bacon.

Combine mayonnaise and next 5 ingredients in small bowl. Mix in reserved bacon drippings. Season with salt and pepper. *(Can be prepared 2 days ahead. Cover dressing and bacon separately and then refrigerate.)*

Combine spinach, mushrooms and eggs in large bowl. Toss with dressing. Sprinkle with bacon and Parmesan and serve.

NEW POTATO SALAD WITH FRESH HERBS

WARM POTATOES ARE tossed with shallots and an herb vinaigrette in this easy-to-make dish.

12 SERVINGS

VINAIGRETTE

3	tablespoons tarragon vinegar or white wine vinegar
1	teaspoon Dijon mustard
1	garlic clove, minced
9	tablespoons olive oil

SALAD

5	pounds new potatoes
3	shallots or green onions, minced
1	cup mayonnaise
1	cup diced celery
¾	cup chopped green onions
¼	cup chopped fresh dill or 1 tablespoon dried
3	tablespoons minced fresh parsley
2	tablespoons chopped fresh chives

FOR VINAIGRETTE: Combine vinegar, mustard and garlic in small bowl. Gradually whisk in oil. Season with salt and pepper.

FOR SALAD: Cover potatoes with salted water in large pot. Cover pot; boil gently just until tender, 15 minutes. Drain. Cool slightly. Slice warm potatoes. Place in large bowl. Toss with vinaigrette and shallots. Let stand 30 minutes.

Mix mayonnaise, celery, green onions, dill, parsley and chives into potatoes. Season to taste with salt and pepper. *(Can be prepared 1 day ahead. Cover and refrigerate.)* Transport salad in plastic container in cooler.

FRESH STRAWBERRY ICE CREAM

CHOCK-FULL OF strawberries, this makes a delightful summer dessert. Store it in a cooler during the clambake. You could also serve wedges of watermelon.

MAKES ABOUT 2¼ QUARTS

3¾	cups sliced fresh strawberries
2¼	cups plus 2 tablespoons sugar
3	tablespoons Grand Marnier
4½	cups whipping cream
1¾	cups plus 2 tablespoons milk
1	vanilla bean, split lengthwise
12	egg yolks

Mix berries, ½ cup sugar and Grand Marnier in medium bowl, crushing berries slightly with spoon. Let stand; stir occasionally.

Combine cream and milk in heavy large saucepan. Scrape in seeds from vanilla bean; add bean. Bring to boil. Reduce heat and simmer 5 minutes. Whisk yolks and remaining 1¾ cups plus 2 tablespoons sugar in large bowl. Gradually whisk in cream mixture. Return to saucepan. Stir over low heat until custard thickens and leaves path on back of spoon when finger is drawn across; do not boil. Strain into large bowl. Cover and refrigerate until well chilled. *(Can be prepared 1 day ahead. Refrigerate strawberries and custard separately.)*

Fold strawberries into custard. Process mixture in ice cream maker according to manufacturer's instructions (in batches if necessary). Freeze ice cream in covered container until firm. *(Can be prepared 3 days ahead.)*

THE REAL THING

A true, traditional New England clambake involves more time than most of us have. But it is, without a doubt, an experience you wouldn't want to miss, given the opportunity. The real thing begins with a large pit dug in the sand at a beach that doesn't prohibit fires. The pit is lined with smooth, round stones, like those found along the shores of New England. A driftwood fire is built atop the rocks, then left to burn for several hours. When the logs have burned down, the hot rocks are topped with a layer of seaweed. The seafood (usually a combination of lobsters and clams), along with corn, is arranged on top of the seaweed, then covered with a water-soaked piece of fishnet or burlap. Then everything steams for about an hour.

The simplified clambake here takes the fresh-seafood-feast idea and applies it to the barbecue, either the kind found at some beaches or the one in your back yard. Wood chips add smoky flavor to the shellfish. If seaweed is available, you could use that too, as a layer between the grill rack and the seafood. Wherever you're picnicking, cover the table with newspaper to encourage messiness, and make sure there are plenty of napkins and cold drinks available.

BON APPÉTIT OUTDOOR ENTERTAINING

ACKNOWLEDGMENTS

The following people contributed recipes included in this book: John Ash; Baker Street, Narberth, Pennsylvania; Lynda Hotch Balslev; Pamela Barefoot; Karen Barker; Melanie Barnard; Nancy Verde Barr; Tom Berthiaume; Betelnut Pejiu Wu, San Francisco, California; Lena Cederham Birnbaum; Bull & Finch Pub, Boston, Massachusetts; Leslie Vaughn Burckard; Misty Callies, Zanzibar, Ann Arbor, Michigan; Kathy Cary; The Cascades Restaurant, Nashville, Tennessee; Sarah and Rives Castleman; Patti and David Cottle; Lane Crowther; Robin Davis; Lori and Jean Louis De Mori; Devora Disner; Brooke Dojny; Kathy and Robert Du Grenier; Adam R. Feerst; Barbara Pool Fenzl; Lisa Ferro; Fifty Seven Fifty Seven Restaurant, New York, New York; Linda and John Finn; Jim Fobel; Millie Pozzo Froeb; Margaret and Stephen Gadient; Beverly Gannon, Hali'imaile General Store, Hali'imaile, Maui, Hawaii; Giuseppe's Italian Cafe, Williamsburg, Virginia; Marcy Goldman; Trish and Jim Gorman; Victoria and Gary Gott; Jim Green; Kathy Gunst; Ken Haedrich; Reed Hearon, Rose Pistola, San Francisco, California; Jessica Hirschman; Russell Ito; Jake's On The Lake, Tahoe City, California; Miles James; Johnson & Wales University, Providence, Rhode Island; Cherryl Kachenmeister; Karen Kaplan; Jeanne Thiel Kelley; Kristine Kidd; Ron Klein; JoAnn and David Krajeski; La Montaña, Steamboat Springs, Colorado; Sam McClure; Tim McClure; Michael McLaughlin; Judi McManigal; Chuck McNeil; Crystal and Bob Moll; Jinx and Jefferson Morgan; Selma Brown Morrow; Gina and Rich Mortillaro; Gina and Jeff Mummery; Rochelle Palermo; Monica Pope, Boulevard Bistrot, Houston, Texas; Red Sage, Washington, D.C.; Louise and Dave Robinson; Peggy Ann Roege; Betty Rosbottom; Cynthia Rowley; Royal Tea Company, Trumbull, Connecticut; Richard Sax; Gina Schild; Kay Schlozman; Oded Schwartz; Tracy Scott; Mary Sellen; Shorty's Mexican Roadhouse, Bedford, New Hampshire; Sharon Shuford; Marie Simmons; Greg Sonnier, Gabrielle Restaurant, New Orleans, Louisiana; Marlena Spieler; Stars, San Francisco, California; Tom Sullivan; Kevin Taylor; Sarah Tenaglia; Charlotte Walker; Dana Walker; Maria Watson; Mike Wilson.

The following people contributed photographs included in this book: Jack Andersen; Noel Barnhurst; David Bishop; Dave Carlin; Wyatt Counts; Julie Dennis; Alison Duke; Beth Galton; Greg Gillis; John Kelly; Brian Leatart; Judd Pilossof; Jeff Sarpa; Elizabeth Watt.

Original photography, front jacket and pages 2/3, 5, 10, 11, 12, 16, 20, 26, 32, 44, 50, 56, 72, 78, 84, 90, 98, 99, 120, 123, 131, 136, 140, 141, 142, 146, 150, 157 158, 162, 168, 173, 174, 178 and 182 by Mark Thomas. *Food stylist:* Rory Spinelli. *Prop stylist:* Nancy Micklin. Additional photography on pages 38, 58, 60 and 66 also by Mark Thomas.

Additional photography on pages 1, 6, 9, 19, 23, 24, 30, 36, 41, 42, 49, 53, 59, 63, 65, 69, 75, 81, 89, 96, 97, 127, 135, 144, 152, 156, 170, 176, 180 and 185 by Jerry Orabona.

SHOPPING DIRECTORY

Page 2: "Hartland" wine goblet, Simon Pierce, 800-774-5277.

Page 20: Flatware from Pottery Barn, 800-922-9934. Sake box by Kotobuki Trading from Ad Hoc Softwares, 212-925-2652.

Page 29: "Talavera" tiles from Mission Tile West, 626-799-4595. "Talavera" platter and bowl from Casa de Sousa, 213-626-7076.

Page 50: Fork from Old Newbury Crafters, 800-343-1388.

Page 66: Table from ABC Carpet & Home, 212-473-3000.

Page 77: Pie plate from Sur La Table, 800-243-0852. Textile by Satin Moon Fabrics, 415-668-1623.

Page 86: Organza napkin from Pottery Barn, 800-922-9934.

Page 90: Trifle bowl and glasses from Pottery Barn, 800-922-9934.

Page 99: Hurricane lamp from Simon Pearce, 800-774-5277.

Page 154: Fluted glass bowl from Crate&Barrel, 888-249-4155.

Page 165: Plate from Dansk, 401-849-4060.

Items not referenced above are privately owned.